BERKELEY'S
PRINCIPLES
OF HUMAN KNOWLEDGE
Critical Studies

WADSWORTH STUDIES IN PHILOSOPHICAL CRITICISM

Alexander Sesonske, General Editor

HUMAN UNDERSTANDING:

Studies in the Philosophy of David Hume

META-*MEDITATIONS*:

Studies in Descartes

PLATO'S *MENO*:

Text and Criticism

PLATO'S *REPUBLIC*:

Interpretation and Criticism

LIMITS OF LIBERTY:

Studies of Mill's *On Liberty*

ARISTOTLE'S *ETHICS*:

Issues and Interpretations

BERKELEY'S
PRINCIPLES OF HUMAN KNOWLEDGE

Critical Studies

BERKELEY'S
PRINCIPLES
OF HUMAN KNOWLEDGE
Critical Studies

edited by

Gale W. Engle
FOOTHILL COLLEGE

&

Gabriele Taylor
ST. ANNE'S COLLEGE
OXFORD UNIVERSITY

Wadsworth Publishing Company, Inc.

BELMONT, CALIFORNIA

WADSWORTH STUDIES IN PHILOSOPHICAL CRITICISM

The idea of a series of Studies in Philosophical Criticism developed in response to a growing problem in American universities. Philosophy can be taught most successfully in small classes; philosophical understanding grows in the course of a dialogue where problems are discussed from diverse points of view by men who differ in experience and temperament. But with the increase in college enrollments, the size of introductory classes has grown larger and the possibility of a dialogue between professor and students more remote. Our hope is that the Studies in Philosophical Criticism will make a dialogue of sorts possible in a class of a hundred, or a thousand, as well as in smaller classes and seminars. Each volume in the series contains a collection of critical writings related to a single classical philosophical text, such as Descartes' *Meditations* or Plato's *Republic*. These critical writings are not substitutes for the classical work, but supplements to it. They should be read in conjunction with the classical text. So used, they will bring to bear on the problems raised by Descartes, Hume, or Plato that diversity of voices and viewpoints which is the heart of the dialogue— and also, we hope, will prompt the student to add his voice to the discussion.

In selecting material for the volumes in the series, the editors have not searched primarily for writings which provide a definitive analysis of the classical text, but have rather selected those papers they thought might be most useful in undergraduate courses in philosophy, both to provoke students into serious engagement with the text and the problems found there, and to present them with a variety of philosophical styles and idioms. Most of the writings reprinted are quite contemporary; they were selected not only for their excellence but also as an indication that many of the classical problems of philosophy persist as centers of current controversy. It is believed that this format also achieves one prime desideratum: it acquaints the student with both the great works of the philosophical tradition and the most contemporary concepts, techniques, and modes of thought.

CONTENTS

INTRODUCTION

In 1685, British empiricist George Berkeley was born in a cottage near Dysert Castle, Thomaston, Ireland. A child of a middle-class family, he was privileged in his education, attending, first, Kilkenny College—not far from Dysert Castle—and second, at the age of 15, Trinity College in Dublin. At Trinity, already a ranking institution, Berkeley gained a command of the classics, acquired an elementary knowledge of Hebrew, informed himself exceptionally well on comtemporary mathematical and physical science, especially the views of Newton, and read John Locke's *Essay Concerning Human Understanding*. After he earned his B.A. degree in 1704, Berkeley stayed on at Trinity to do graduate study; and in 1707 he was made a Fellow of his college on the condition of his taking clerical orders.

Almost immediately he began his philosophical writings. His notebooks of 1707–1709[1] clearly indicate his precociousness and his marked progress toward a mature philosophical position. And over the next four years, he produced three of his most important publications: *Essay Towards a New Theory of Vision* (1709); *A Treatise Concerning the Principles of Human Knowledge* (1710); and *Three Dialogues Between Hylas and Philonous* (1713).

Of these early publications, the *Principles* has been chosen for consideration in this collection of expository and critical essays because it contains most of the seminal doctrines of Berkeley's theory of knowledge and its related metaphysics. And in spite of the bad press given this work during Berkeley's lifetime, it is now regarded as his major philosophical effort. Berkeley himself was undismayed by the attacks of his critics; he was certain that his doctrines, arrived at before he was twenty-three years old and but slightly modified later, provided the key to a range of philosophical puzzles.

Berkeley examined philosophical themes that particularly command the attention of his twentieth-century successors: language and thought, words and signs, primary and secondary qualities, substance, universals and particulars, understanding and will, mind and other

---

[1] Referred to by Fraser in 1871 as the *Commonplace Book* and by Jessop and Luce, in 1957, as the *Philosophical Commentaries*.

minds, and causation and God. The essays in this volume were chosen because they discuss most of the significant Berkeleian topics, and because they reflect many of the controversies and puzzles that Berkeley inherited and dealt with.

The following pages of this Introduction draw the reader's attention to the key interpretations and arguments of the twelve contributors to this book. The discussion of these contributions is divided, like the book, into five of the problem areas of Berkeley's philosophy in the *Principles:* Minds and Ideas, Perception and Existence, Philosophy and Science, Primary and Secondary Qualities, and Berkeley and God.

Minds and Ideas. The problem S. A. Grave raises in his essay "The Mind and Its Ideas" is based largely on two fundamental principles in Berkeley's philosophy. These are (1) the Identity Principle, which maintains that the things we see and feel are "but so many sensations, notions, ideas or impressions on the sense;" and (2) the Distinction Principle, which states that the mind and its ideas are entirely distinct. The consequences and implications of these two principles seem hard to reconcile, for while (1) bases the existence of things on their perception by an individual perceiver, (2) leads to the view that things depend on God for their existence but are independent of any human perceiver. Like the status of things, the status of the perceiving mind varies according to which principle we use to interpret the *esse est percipere* doctrine. For either the mind is nothing apart from its mental operations (the Identity Principle) or the mind is something apart from its thinking but is as a matter of course always engaged in some mental operation (the Distinction Principle).

Grave believes that Berkeley is arguing against the doctrine that the self is a system of floating ideas and that he is therefore putting forward a substantivalist account of the mind. C. M. Turbayne, on the other hand, in his article "Berkeley's Two Concepts of Mind," agrees that this substantivalist account is indeed one theory of mind in the *Principles* but argues that there is another, non-substantivalist, account at least latent in Berkeley's writings. The support for this thesis is based largely on Turbayne's unconventional interpretation of the *Principles.* Turbayne suggests that Berkeley uses his destructive analyses of the common philosophical sources of error—category mistakes, abstract ideas, proper names, and especially metaphors—to make credible his hinted non-substantivalist theory of mind.

Berkeley thought that the source of error in some doctrines, such as materialism and representationalism, was a theory of meaning which led to the doctrine of abstract ideas. There is, according to him, a necessary connection between materialism and abstract ideas, and, conversely, there is a necessary connection between the theory that there are no such ideas and his own doctrine of immaterialism. Monroe C. Beardsley, in "Berkeley on Abstract Ideas," questions the justification of Berkeley's claim that his attack on abstraction is an essential basis for his positive doctrine. He concludes (1) that when Berkeley invokes the attack on abstract ideas in order to support his immaterialism, his argument sometimes depends on the Identity Principle and has nothing to do with abstraction; and (2) that where the abstract idea argument is apparently legitimately used to refute Realism, Berkeley runs into inconsistencies elsewhere.

Perception and Existence. In "Physical Objects as Permanent Possibilities of Sensation," J. S. Mill defends a theory of the external world which is compatible with *one* possible interpretation of Berkeley's doctrine—that what we call the external world is not made up of what we actually perceive but rather of the aggregate of possibilities of sensation. Mill thus proposes an analysis of physical-object statements in terms of counter-factuals: "If I were suddenly transported to the banks of the Hoogly, I should still have the sensations which, if now present, would lead me to affirm that Calcutta exists here and now." Such a theory would, in Mill's view, account for our concept of matter; for the aggregate of possible sensations is permanent, whereas actual sensations are fleeting. Further, this aggregate is independent of individual perceivers, whereas particular sensations are observer-dependent. The belief that matter is something over and above permanent possibilities of sensation Mill traces back to the mistaken step from "any one sensation is different from any one physical object" to "the sum total of sensations is different from the external world." Thus the supposition that Berkeley shared Mill's view depends to a large extent on one's interpretation of Berkeley's *esse est percipi* principle.

Konrad Marc-Wogau, in "Berkeley's Sensationalism and the *Esse Est Percipi*-Principle," makes a detailed examination of this principle and offers two formulations: (x) (x exists ≡ x is perceived) and (x) (x exists ⊃ x is perceived). The second formula expresses Berkeley's Idealism. It is weaker than the first, which is the conjunction of the second formula with (x)(x is perceived ⊃ x exists), which in turn expresses the thesis that the object of sense-perception is undoubtedly real, or exists. (x) (x exists $\equiv$ x is perceived) therefore implies both Berkeley's Idealism and what might be called his thesis of the infallibility of sense-perception. Two points are of importance in connection with Marc-Wogau's formulations: (1) Neither formulation gives us precise information as to the relation between *esse* and *percipi;* they leave it open, for example, whether it is analytically (and if so, definitionally) true that to exist is to be perceived, or merely contingently true; (2) There are occasions when the validity of Berkeley's arguments depends on an oscillation between the two formulations.

The formulation (x) (x exists $\supset$ x is perceived) is clearly of crucial importance to Berkeley, and Marc-Wogau examines several interpretations of one central argument designed to establish this position. The argument refers to the peculiar situation of being able to imagine, for example, oranges on a tree and nobody to perceive them; but the one who does the imagining must perceive them or think of them all the time: "Although nobody is imagined to perceive the ideas, they are nevertheless perceived." Berkeley, however, holds that it is contradictory to imagine or to perceive ideas as not perceived. Therefore no ideas exist unperceived. Marc-Wogau finds logical faults in all the interpretations of this argument, but favors the fifth, which follows from these premises:

1. A proposition p must be considered as certain or proved if the supposition of its negation ("I suppose that p is false") is a contradiction.
2. To suppose something about x implies to perceive x.
3. The proposition "I suppose that x is unperceived" implies that x is unperceived.

Marc-Wogau does, however, state two important objections to this more probable interpretation.

David Hume, in "Of Personal Identity," ignores the ordinary ways of establishing particular identity—for example, giving, descriptions of bodies and their actions—and restricts himself to the internal world. He tries to justify the claim that there is a self, or mind, that is not only identifiable but retains the same identity through time. He rests his case on theories of impressions, memory, imagination, resemblance, and causation.

For Hume all impressions are separate and distinct; impressions cause images, and these, retained by memory, are augmented by imagination to create the conviction that we have particular identity. The Humean analysis has been attacked many times, and Hume himself was aware of his failure to make a case for personal identity. Thus, Hume deserves credit for being prepared to abandon his conclusions, even though, as a criticism of Berkeley's "mental substance," Hume's unrealistic conception of the self is not particularly convincing.

R. M. Chisholm's "Phenomenalism" establishes a link between Berkeley's "perception-existence" theory and its twentieth-century counterpart. Berkeley argued that all we experience are ideas (sense data). We do not experience material objects, nor are our ideas caused by objects existing independently of minds. A direct act of God's will causes us to have ideas (sense data) in our minds. Moreover, objects are aggregates of ideas or sense qualities. That is, knowledge of objects is a knowledge of the qualities and relationships of subjective experience. Here Berkeley was attacking Locke's contention that there are material objects existing independently of minds and that these objects cause the content of our sense-experience.

Berkeley's interpretation has been referred to as phenomenalistic because he anticipated the twentieth-century proponents of phenomenalism, who reduce everything to phenomena, or appearances. If we were to ask "What is an artichoke?", the Berkeleian answer would be that it is an aggregate of ideas (sense data). The modern counterpart would hold that the material-object statement "This thing is an artichoke" is expressible in sets of statements referring solely to sense data. Chisholm considers this claim false. In his view there is no logical entailment between a given material-object statement and a set of statements referring solely to appearances (sense data). He argues that only under special circumstances is an appearance-statement entailed by a thing-statement. For example, in order for the thing-statement "This is red" to entail an appearance-statement "Redness will be sensed," there must be a further statement referring to observation conditions—for example, "This is perceived under normal conditions; and if this is red and is perceived under normal conditions, redness will be sensed."

Philosophy and Science. In the *Principles*, Berkeley gave a prominent place to philosophy of science and also anticipated important developments of the twentieth century. In later works, notably *De Motu*, he carried forward his critique of science. In "A Note on Berkeley as Precursor of Mach and Einstein," Sir Karl Popper organizes the evidence that confirms Berkeley's status as a philosopher of science. Moreover, he underscores the phenomenalism which Berkeley and Mach hold in common, Berkeley's theism being the only significant difference between them.

T. E. Jessop's article, "Berkeley's Philosophy of Science," reinforces Popper with an articulate description of Berkeley's theories on science. Both Popper and Jessop note that Berkeley's main attack in the *Principles* is on Newton's dynamics. Berkeley wants men of science to stay within the empirical bounds of their subject. Such words as *force* are only "mathematical hypotheses," useful for "reckoning and mathematical demonstration" but not for metaphysics. Concepts of space, time, and motion are wrongly modified by the word *absolute;* space, time, and motion are relative terms. Causal connections are only empirical uniformities, not necessary ones. To limit corporeal happenings to mechanical causes is not only to fail to understand causal connection but also to eliminate the real causal agents: minds—those of humans and that of God.

Primary and Secondary Qualities. Thomas Reid, in "Of the Objects of Perception," and Jonathan Bennett, in "Substance, Reality, and Primary Qualities," both defend the distinction between primary and secondary qualities against Berkeley's attack. Reid follows Locke in distinguishing between qualities of bodies and sensations; he locates one source of confusion in some of Berkeley's interpretations of the doctrine: the label "secondary quality" is sometimes attached to the quality of the body itself and sometimes to the sensation produced by the quality in a sentient being. Given this, Reid defends three theses:

1. Berkeley is mistaken in his interpretation of the Lockean doctrine.

2. If secondary qualities are to be regarded as properties of objects, then they are the causes of our sensations. We can know and describe our sensations, but we cannot know and describe their causes. Primary qualities, by contrast, can be known perfectly and are the objects of the mathematical sciences.

3. If, alternatively, we regard secondary qualities not as the unknown causes of our sensations but as the sensations themselves (for example, green, sweet), then it is clear that bodies cannot possess secondary qualities independent of a sentient observer. Primary qualities, however, being properties of bodies, do not depend on the perceiver for their existence.

Bennett agrees with Reid's first thesis and elaborates it, distinguishing three separate doctrines which, he claims, are confused in Berkeley's interpretation. Bennett might also be said to agree with Reid's third thesis, in that he argues that there is a set of qualities essentially related to a body's connection with and reaction to other bodies, which separates the primary from the secondary qualities.

Berkeley and God. The question at issue between Jonathan Bennett, in "Berkeley and God," and E. J. Furlong, in "Berkeley and the Tree in the Quad," concerns the precise role of God in Berkeley's philosophy. Both authors ask two different kinds of question: (1) the historical one: What did Berkeley himself believe this role to be? (2) the logical one: What justification did Berkeley have for his beliefs, and how valid are the arguments he puts forward in support of them? Bennett argues that, legitimately or not, Berkeley considers God the cause of our ideas; for all ideas have causes, and since at least some of the ideas we have are not caused by us, they must be caused by a superior being. Bennett doubts that Berkeley was much concerned with the other alleged function of God: to provide for the continuity of objects when unperceived by man. Bennett and Furlong differ on this interpretation of Berkeley's position rather than about the logical status of his arguments.

We have been privileged to question many people concerning the need for this book and the essays to be included. For encouragement, advice, and suggestions, we are in debt to Professors E. J. Furlong, J. D. Goheen, D. Mitchell, A. Sesonske, G. J. Warnock, and G. Ryle. Mrs. Gale Engle's care in typing and preparing the manuscript was invaluable.

MINDS AND IDEAS

THE MIND AND ITS IDEAS:
SOME PROBLEMS
IN THE INTERPRETATION
OF BERKELEY*

S. A. Grave

The problems of interpretation with which I shall be concerned are set by what Berkeley says (1) about the relation of ideas to the mind, (2) about the mind itself.

I

The mind and its ideas, Berkeley states, are "entirely distinct."[1] This, I think, is the basic text for the unparadoxical Berkeley presented by Professor A. A. Luce; it states, at any rate, a position presupposed by this Berkeley's other opinions. He still maintains, of course, that physical things are "collections of ideas" and that ideas are "in the mind." But what does "in the mind" mean? It will mean something consistent with the entire distinction of ideas from the mind. "My meaning," Berkeley says, "is only that the mind comprehends or perceives them. . . ."[2] By "in the mind," Luce says, Berkeley means (with some colouring according to its context) "in direct cognitive relation to the mind."[3] There is nothing in this relationship which anchors the being of ideas to their being perceived by anyone in particular rather than by someone else. The things they constitute are therefore freed from dependence on any of us, being denied merely an existence "exterior" to all minds. Different perceivers can perceive the same things, which, in our absence, are sustained in existence as objects of God's never-failing "perception."

* From *The Australasian Journal of Philosophy*, XLII, (1964), 199–210. Reprinted by permission of the editors of *The Australasian Journal of Philosophy*.

[1] *The Principles of Human Knowledge*, sec. 2, sec. 89. Quotations from Berkeley are from A. A. Luce–T. E. Jessop edition of *Works* (Nelson, 1948–57). Section references only from *Principles*.

[2] *Three Dialogues between Hylas and Philonous*, III (*Works*, vol. 2, p. 250). *Prin.*, sec. 2.

[3] "Berkeley's Existence in the Mind," *Mind*, July, 1941, p. 260.

Berkeley has supplied all the materials for this unparadoxical Berkeley, whose doctrine is indeed so little extraordinary that, apart from making all agency volitional, it differs only in queer expression from the assertions of ordinary theism. The physical world has no existence independently of God. But this is equally true of finite minds. The dependence of every physical thing on being perceived subsides, when no perceiver is indispensable except God, into the dependence of everything on God.

Shortly after declaring the mind and its ideas to be entirely distinct, Berkeley asks of "the things we see and feel": "what are they but so many sensations, notions, ideas or impressions on the sense; and is it possible to separate, even in thought, any of these from perception?" And he answers: "For my part I might as easily divide a thing from it self."[4] The identity of an idea with the perception of it welds ideas to individual perceivers, with the following consequences. The "same idea which is in my mind, cannot be in yours"—as Berkeley's Hylas says;[5] since things are collections of ideas, you and I therefore never perceive the self-same thing. The things each of us perceives have an intermittent existence with the intermittency of our perception and no existence before our perception of them or after this has ceased. The possibility of a physical world to which God's "perception" is necessary and all other perception indifferent, is quite ruled out.

We have, then, as regards the perceptual access of different individuals to the same object, and as regards the conditions under which physical things exist, two sets of opinions, both of which might very plausibly be ascribed to Berkeley on the basis of what he asserts or implies. We shall be asking presently whether Berkeley inconsistently held both sets of opinions; if not, which of them he really held, and how the illusory presence of the other is to be explained.

Corresponding to these two sets of opinions are the two principles which I am calling, respectively, the "distinction" and "identity" principles. The "distinction-principle" would permit the unparadoxical opinions; the "identity-principle," itself paradoxical, would require the paradoxical opinions. Nothing would be more valuable in Berkelian commentary than a reconciliation of these principles, an interpretation of Berkeley's words about the entire distinction of minds and ideas,

---

[4] *Prin.*, sec. 5.
[5] *Three Dialogues*, III (*Works*, vol. 2, p. 247).

which would show that he had a meaning for them consistent with what he says about the identity of an idea and its perception. I regret having no suggestions to offer. The positions seem to me quite irreconcilable, and I think Berkeley was driven into them by two conflicting desires: one, to oblige men to see that if there were no minds there would be nothing at all; the other, to meet the demands of common sense.

"Mem: To be eternally banishing Metaphisics & recalling Men to Common Sense," Berkeley wrote in his Note Books.[6] He will not allow, of course, that his own metaphysical enterprise runs into difficulties with common sense; he thinks he can always secure the non-resistance of common sense when he cannot have its aid. But good relations with common sense require that the objects of sight, touch, hearing, etc. be kept distinct from the mind. An entry in the Note Books reads fairly plainly as giving the necessary assurance: "I will grant you that extension, colour, etc. may be said to be without the Mind in a double respect i.e. as independent of our Will & as distinct from the Mind."[7]

I have suggested that a concern for common sense demanded from Berkeley the distinction-principle. His metaphysical enterprise could not do without the identity-principle. Why do physical things have to be perceived in order to exist? The distinction-principle, which would counter any answer, has dropped out of sight when the question is raised. Berkeley's sustained effort to prove that physical things have no being when not perceived, is to be found in arguments designed to reduce physical things to sensible things, sensible things to arrangements of sensible qualities, sensible qualities to sensations or ideas, in which what one is aware of can no more be separated from one's awareness of it, than a thing can be detached from itself.

Let us now remind ourselves of the consequences of the identity-principle. It requires each of us as different perceivers to perceive different things. It prohibits the things that each of us perceives from existing before our perception of them and imposes on them an intermittent existence with the intermittency of our perception. It rules out the possibility of a physical world sustained by God alone. Some sense of Berkeley's commitment to these consequences rarely escapes his readers, but though he occasionally gives them oblique expression, he

[6] *Philosophical Commentaries*, 751.
[7] *Philosophical Commentaries*, 882.

does not avow them; on the contrary, he appears repeatedly, in explicit words or by implication, to represent them as misunderstandings of his position; the opinions that he appears to declare are the unparadoxical ones that the distinction-principle would sanction. Thus there appear to be two Berkeleys in Berkeley, one of them—discernible largely by inference and interpretation—conforming to the prescriptions of the identity-principle, the other—very visible—availing himself of the permissions of the distinction-principle. The first principle, it might be suggested, would operate in the construction of Berkeley's theory, the second in its defence against common sense objections.

I shall try to show that these appearances are altogether deceptive: that Berkeley never repudiated any of the consequences of the identity-principle; that the distinction-principle is in complete abeyance when the question is asked whether the perception of different individuals can have a common object, and when issues are raised as to the conditions under which physical things exist; that the illusion of two conflicting sets of opinions is generated by the expression of paradoxical opinions in unparadoxical language.

Berkeley argues in the Third Dialogue that he maintains nothing that would prevent us from saying that different persons are perceiving the same thing, whenever this is what we would ordinarily say: the word "same" is applied "where no distinction or variety is perceived," and he is not altering anyone's "perceptions."

Let us suppose several men together, all endued with the same faculties, and consequently affected in like sort by their senses, and who had yet never known the use of language; they would without question agree in their perceptions. Though perhaps, when they came to the use of speech, some regarding the uniformness of what was perceived, might call it the *same* thing: others especially regarding the diversity of persons who perceived, might choose the denomination of different things. But who sees not that all the dispute is about a word? to wit, whether what is perceived by different persons, may yet have the term *same* applied to it?

These imaginary men suddenly endowed with speech are presented as speaking like ordinary men; the point of the conjectural experiment is that what they say might naturally be said by anybody in their situation. The first group say: "We all perceive the same thing." (That they are really no ordinary men is indicated by the fact that, as Berkeley has it, this is only what they *might* say.) The second group are astonishingly disposed to affirm that different things are perceived—not because of any feature of what is perceived, for they are all "affected in like sort by their senses," but because there are several perceivers. This consideration, together with Berkeley's comment that "same" or "different" here is a matter of words in the choice of which one can please oneself, shows how what the first group say is to be construed: different persons can perceive the same thing in the sense in which they can have the same headache (or the same idea, in the ordinary sense of "idea"). Neither group is composed of ordinary men: the second consists of Berkelians voicing paradox, the first of Berkelians concealing it.

Berkeley concludes the discussion of his problem with a casual gesture towards divine "archetypes," not themselves perceived by us but corresponding to the objects of our perception. He points out that the objection that "no two see the same thing" bears no more hardly on him than on the philosophers who hold the kind of theory Locke held. They acknowledge that we immediately perceive only our own ideas. "But they suppose," he has Hylas say, "an external archetype, to which referring their several ideas, they may truly be said to perceive the same thing." Hylas is assured that the "principles" he is being invited to accept also allow the supposition that our ideas have external archetypes. External to our minds, located in the divine mind, they serve "all the ends of identity" as effectively as if they had absolute externality. A poor recommendation, as Hylas must have known unless he had quite forgotten the close of the First Dialogue.

Samuel Johnson, Berkeley's American correspondent, wrote to him raising difficulties about a number of matters and wanting to be sure that he always had Berkeley's meaning. On the basis of deliberate remarks which we shall be considering presently, he had understood Berkeley to be assigning a double-aspect existence to things, giving them an archetypal being as ideas in the divine mind, and an ectypal being in finite minds as ideas "copying" or "imaging" or "resembling" in some way these exemplars. "When therefore," Johnson wrote, "several people are said to see the same tree or star, etc. . . . it is (if I understand you) *unum et idem in archetypo*, tho' *multiplex et diversum in ectypo*, for it is as evident that your idea is not mine nor mine yours when we say we both look on the same tree, as that you are not I, nor I you."[8] Berkeley's reply to Johnson is silent on this point.

How are we to understand Berkeley's assurances that our percep-

---

[8] Second letter to Berkeley (*Works*, vol. 2, p. 286).

tion does not affect the existence of things? We have to go on hints and obscure statements, but there is enough to let it be seen that Berkeley is not repudiating any of the consequences of the identity-principle, that he is speaking with the vulgar, however reluctantly he may be only speaking with them. Several ways of thinking are open to the learned in this matter, as they are when different perceivers are said to perceive the same thing. One of them, which reappears fugitively but without disguise in the *Principles*, is indicated in the Note Books, with Berkeley's reminder to himself of the need for undisturbing words:

Mem: to allow existence to colours in the dark, persons not thinking &c but not an absolute actual existence. 'Tis prudent to correct mens mistakes without altering their language. This makes truth glide into their souls insensibly.

Colours in the dark do exist really *i.e.* were there light or as soon as light comes we shall see them provided we open our eyes. & that whether we will or no.[9]

There is another suggestion in the Note Books. It is directly applicable to Berkeley's insistence that things have an existence "exterior" to our minds in the mind of God: "+ Bodies etc. do exist even when not perceiv'd they being powers in the active Being."[10] One has to avoid propping up an interpretation of Berkeley with anything doubtful from his Note Books, anything that he could plausibly be regarded as having repudiated during their composition. Entries inconsistent with later entries come into this class, along with those bearing the + sign which Berkeley might have intended as a cancelling mark. Most of the entries reducing, or appearing to reduce, unperceived objects to powers carry the + sign, but a self-admonition towards the end of the Note Books removes any disqualification on this score: "Not to mention the Combinations of Powers but to say the things the effects themselves to really exist even when not actually perceiv'd but still with relation to perception."[11] The most natural construction to be put on this remark would seem to be that Berkeley has decided against revealing an opinion which he has not rejected.[12]

---

[9] *Philosophical Commentaries*, 185, 185a; cf. *Prin.*, sec. 3, 58.
[10] *Philosophical Commentaries*, 52; cf. 41, 282, 293, 293a.
[11] *Philosophical Commentaries*, 802.
[12] *Three Dialogues*, III (*Works*, vol. 2, pp. 239–40).

We are to say that the things we perceive exist independently of our perception of them. The suggestions just mentioned provide possibilities of meaning for our words when we are speaking not only with strict propriety but also according to the truth of things. Berkeley suggests yet a further possibility: the things we perceive exist independently of us in their divine archetypes. He cannot, of course, allow us to perceive the divine archetypes themselves. To suppose that anything we perceive is identical with anything in God is to corporealize deity. And so he says, repudiating Malebranche's "notion" of our *"seeing all things in God"*: "I do not understand how our ideas, which are things altogether passive and inert, can be the essence, or any part (or like any part) of the essence or substance of God, who is an impassive, indivisible, purely active being."[13] Berkeley goes on to state what he declares to be his own position:

Take here in brief my meaning. It is evident that the things I perceive are my own ideas, and that no idea can exist unless it be in a mind. Nor is it less plain that these ideas or things by me perceived, either themselves or their archetypes, exist independently of my mind, since I know myself not to be their author, it being out of my power to determine at pleasure, what particular ideas I shall be affected with upon opening my eyes or ears. They must therefore exist in some other mind, whose will it is they should be exhibited to me.

It is an odd statement. The things one perceives are one's own ideas, Berkeley says. We draw the inferences: therefore no one else's (in virtue of the identity-principle, necessarily no one else's), therefore with no existence independently of their perceiver's mind. These things, Berkeley says, or their archetypes (as though it didn't matter which) exist independently of their perceiver in some other mind. We do not take the alternatives seriously: it is of course the archetypes which exist in another mind, and are "exhibited" when things are perceived. Whatever this word might mean, it cannot, consistently with Berkeley's criticism of Malebranche, mean "exhibited."

We perceive objects of sense; the divine archetypes cannot become objects to our senses. What we perceive was brought into existence: the divine archetypes are eternal and uncreated. Arguing in the Third Dialogue for the compatibility of his opinions with the scriptural account of creation,[14] Berkeley sets up a "two-fold state of

---

[13] *Three Dialogues*, II (*Works*, vol. 2, pp. 213–14). cf. *Prin.*, sec. 148.
[14] *Works*, vol. 2, pp. 250–56. cf. Letter to Percival, *Works*, vol. 8, pp. 37–38.

things, the one ectypal or natural . . . created in time," "the other archetypal and eternal." This, he implies, will give everybody all he can intelligibly want. We are bound in theological orthodoxy to assert that "all objects are eternally known by God." Berkeley asserts it, with the remark that to say that they have "an eternal existence" in the mind of God, is to state the same truth. According to the doctrine of creation, the things that make up the physical world have a beginning. And according to Berkeley also, they have a beginning—relatively to finite perceivers, for "nothing is new, or begins to be, in respect of the mind of God." The creative decree, by which the physical world was brought into existence, made "perceptible" to creatures what was previously hidden in deity.

Berkeley has Hylas put the objection that he is allowing things which in the Mosaic history of creation precede man, "no actuality of absolute existence" but only "hypothetical being," before there were men to perceive them. There is no inconsistency between his opinions and the Mosaic history, Berkeley replies: these things might have existed before men in the minds of "other created intelligences."

I say farther, in case we conceive the Creation, as we should at this time a parcel of plants or vegetables of all sorts, produced by an invisible power, in a desert where no body was present: that this way of explaining or conceiving it, is consistent with my principles, since they deprive you of nothing, either sensible or imaginable: that it exactly suits with the common, natural, undebauched notions of mankind . . . I say moreover, that in this naked conception of things, divested of words, there will not be found any notion of what you call the *actuality of absolute existence.*

Berkeley's contention here seems to be this: for men of plain, uncorrupted common sense, a thing exists if it could be perceived by anyone suitably circumstanced; they have no use for, and find no meaning in, talk about "actuality of absolute existence."

To sum up. Berkeley did not hold two sets of conflicting opinions, governed by the identity and distinction principles respectively; he held the opinions prescribed by the identity-principle. He would like to have been, and was willing to be thought, a theistic realist; he was a theistic phenomenalist. These are the metaphysical facts as Berkeley sees them: without God nothing at all would exist; without creatures capable of perception nothing physical would exist, for physical things are constituted by ideas of sense which God "excites" in the mind or "imprints" upon it; without X nothing that X perceives would exist, for the things he perceives are constituted by his ideas. But there are correspondences between X's ideas and Y's, and between their ideas and the divine archetypal ideas. The metaphysical facts have no implications for our actual or possible experience. Accordingly, Berkeley thought, acceptance of his opinions called for no paradoxical language: we are to continue to say in the ordinarily appropriate circumstances that different perceivers perceive the same thing, and to speak in a manner that implies that things are unaffected by our perception of them.

II

I now turn to problems of interpretation that arise in connection with some features of Berkeley's conception of the mind.

Besides our ideas, there is "something which knows or perceives them, and exercises divers operations, as willing, imagining, remembering about them. This perceiving, active being is what I call *mind*, *spirit, soul* or *my self*."[15] "A spirit is one simple, undivided, active being: as it perceives ideas, it is called the *understanding*, and as it produces or otherwise operates about them, it is called the *will*."[16] We shall be particularly concerned with the elucidation of these statements which represent the mind as a substance, as something, that is, to which its actions and passions belong, which is single, simple, and enduring, while they are various and transitory. The substantival mind (the soul, the self) is not, for Berkeley, an occult entity whose existence is merely a suppositional necessity. It is not an unknowable substratum of experience but something of which one is, or can become, "conscious." The word "substance" does not appear in either of the passages before us. If Berkeley rather tended to avoid speaking of the mind as a substance—except, curiously, in relation to ideas which he did *not* think of as modifications of a substance—it was perhaps because the word with its Lockian associations so strongly suggested an unknowable substratum.

Berkeley asserts that the qualities which constitute physical things, deprived of the impossible "support" of material substance, have instead the "support" of immaterial substance, that the mind is

15 *Prin.*, sec. 2.
16 *Prin.*, sec. 27.

their "subject" or "substratum."[17] All the familiar metaphysical words, and all their familiar implications are cancelled or radically changed. "It is therefore evident there can be no *substratum* of those qualities but spirit, in which they exist . . ." The distinction-principle, usually inert when the dependence of ideas upon the mind is in question, now controls Berkeley's meaning and he completes his sentence with the words "not by way of mode or property, but as a thing perceived in that which perceives it."[18] Not by way of mode or property, because, as he explains, if such were the manner of their presence, extension, colour, etc., would be predicable of the mind;[19] the mind could be red and round.

Now if we look for the reasons Berkeley gives for holding the mind to be a substance, I think that, apart from one short argument, and the vague and perfunctory experiential claim that he is "conscious" of his being, that he knows it by "a reflex act," we shall not find anything other than fragmentary expression of the need for a "support" or "subject" of ideas. And we have just seen that, for Berkeley, the mind does not stand to its ideas as a substance to its modes and qualities; that to say that the mind supports its ideas or is their subject is merely to say that ideas, in order to exist, must be perceived. It seems so far an open question whether ideas must be perceived by what has the monadic unity of a substance, or whether it is sufficient that they occur as items in a "congeries of perceptions." We might profitably at this point consider Berkeley's short argument.

Your denial of material substance, Hylas says to Philonous, should commit you, in consistency, to the opinion that you yourself are "only a system of floating ideas, without any substance to support them." The answer he gets is this: Material substance cannot be perceived, is not even conceivable. But "I know or am conscious of my own being . . . I know that I, one and the same self, perceive both colours and sounds: that a colour cannot perceive a sound, nor a sound a colour: that I am therefore one individual principle, distinct from colour and sound; and, for the same reason, from all other sensible things and inert ideas."[20]

Though Berkeley speaks metaphorically when he asserts that ideas and the things they constitute have their "support," "subject,"

[17] *Prin.*, sec. 89, 91; *Three Dialogues*, III (*Works*, vol. 2, pp. 233, 237).

[18] *Three Dialogues*, III (*Works*, vol. 2, p. 237).

[19] *Prin.*, sec. 49.

[20] *Three Dialogues*, III (*Works*, vol. 2, pp. 233–34).

"substratum" in the mind, he is clearly not dealing in metaphor in this argument for the mind or self as a substance, as something unifying its experience itself an uncompounded unity, not a "system" but "one individual principle." And the literal truth of a substantialist account of the mind seems to be presupposed in his argument for the immortality of the soul: "indivisible, incorporeal . . . an active, simple, uncompounded substance," the soul is invulnerable to the decay and dissolution which affects bodies and is therefore immortal by nature.[21]

Once again, however, we have to consider the possibility of a divided, or of a disguised, Berkeley. The functions of the mind as substance are certainly more abridged for Berkeley than is often supposed: he does not regard the mind's ideas as its "accidents." But the actions and passions of the mind must belong to it as accidents belong to their substance, if the word "substance" ever retains its standard meaning as a metaphysical term when he applies it to the mind. A characterization of the mind which is to be found in both the *Principles* and the *Three Dialogues*, some entries in the Note Books, and an evasiveness in the correspondence with Johnson suggest that he might be merely retaining the word while holding a conception of the mind which would properly be called anti-substantialist.

". . . all the unthinking objects of the mind agree, in that they are entirely passive, and their existence consists only in being perceived: whereas a soul or spirit is an active being, whose existence consists not in being perceived, but in perceiving ideas and thinking."[22] How are we meant to understand the parallel asserted here between the relation of an object to its being perceived and the relation of a subject to its perceiving? When *esse est percipi* is construed according to the identity-principle, there is not both the object *and* its being perceived—these are one and the same. Are we to construe *esse est percipere* similarly; or are we to apply an equivalent of the distinction-principle and take Berkeley to mean not that "perceiving ideas and thinking" constitute the being of their subject, but that their subject has no inert being, that it is always perceiving and thinking?

If we turn to the Note Books for illumination, we find Berkeley in a late entry toppling the substantival pronoun into the verb: "Substance of a Spirit is that it acts, causes, wills, operates, or if you

---

[21] *Prin.*, sec. 141.
[22] *Prin.*, sec. 139; cf. sec. 71, sec. 81 and *Three Dialogues*, II (*Works*, vol. 2, p. 223).

please (to avoid the quibble that may be made on the word it) to act, cause, will, operate . . ."[23] On the other hand, the set of "Humian" entries (" . . . Mind is a congeries of Perceptions . . .")[24] is marked with the + sign. And there are several late entries which more or less clearly assert the mind to have a being not constituted by its willing and perceiving. This is the most explicit of them: "I must not Mention the Understanding as a faculty or part of the Mind, I must include Understanding & Will etc. in the word Spirit by which I mean all that is active. I must not say that the Understanding differs not from the particular Ideas, or the Will from particular Volitions."[25] Two entries occurring well on in the Note Books present a specific problem of interpretation:

Certainly the mind always & constantly thinks & we know this too In Sleep & trances the mind exists not there is no time no succession of Ideas.

To say the mind exists without thinking is a Contradiction, nonsense, nothing.[26]

Is it a contradiction to suppose that the mind exists without "thinking" because the mind *is* its thinking, or because to exist it must persist through time, and there is no time without the succession of ideas in thinking? When Berkeley asserts in *Principles*, §98, "that the soul always thinks," the reason given is one which connects the "duration" of finite minds with this succession, and we are not helped towards an understanding of *esse est percipere* where Berkeley adds that anyone attempting to "abstract the *existence* of a spirit from its *cogitation*" will find it a difficult task.

If "*esse* be only *percipere*," Samuel Johnson wrote, he could not understand how Berkeley framed the argument for the immortality of the soul. And wouldn't the soul have more being at one time and less at another, corresponding to variations in the intensity of its "thinking"? And "if *esse* be only *percipere*, upon what is our consciousness founded? I perceived yesterday, and I perceive now, but last night between my yesterday's and today's perception there has been an intermission when I perceived nothing. It seems to me there must be some principle common to these perceptions, whose *esse* don't depend

[23] *Philosophical Commentaries*, 829.
[24] *Ibid.*, 579–81.
[25] *Ibid.*, 848; cf. 849, 871.
[26] *Ibid.*, 651, 652.

upon them, but in which they are, as it were, connected, and on which they depend, whereby I am and continue conscious of them."[27] Since "any degree of perception" is "sufficient to Existence," Berkeley replied, it does not follow that we have more existence at one time than at another; a thousand yards of snow is not whiter than a yard. He contrasted Locke who "holds an abstract idea of existence; exclusive of perceiving and being perceived" with Descartes who "proceeds upon other principles."[28] He did not mention the argument for the immortality of the soul. He directed Johnson to examine carefully what he had said in various places about abstraction.

What he had said about abstraction does nothing to determine whether or not its "absurdity" is incurred in supposing the soul to be other than its perceptions and volitions, though never without some one or other of these. To try to separate the being of sensible things from their being perceived is to attempt an impossible abstraction, but we attempt it also if we try to imagine extension without any of the secondary qualities—though extension is different from these qualities. Yet if Berkeley did hold a substantialist doctrine of the soul, how are we to explain the evasiveness of his replies to Johnson? If he did not, how are we to understand his argument for the immortality of the soul?[29] And how are we to interpret the description of the soul or mind as "an active, simple, uncompounded substance," as "one simple undivided, active being?"

Esse est percipere, on one interpretation of this formula, resolves the mind into the complexity of its active and passive experience. *Esse est percipi*, intended to define the existence of bodies, has consequences for the mind that are more radical. The ideas of sense which constitute corporeal things have no being unperceived because their being is their being perceived. These ideas, Berkeley explains, are not in the mind "by way of mode"; their presence in that manner would corporealize the mind; that they are "in the mind" means only that they are perceived. If, however, an idea and the perception of an idea are identical, it is impossible for perception to be a modification of the mind. Unless *esse est percipi* is understood according to the distinction-principle, so that being and being perceived are merely (and gratuitously) hyphenated, perception seems to sheer off from its subject and to collapse into its objects. "Wherein," to repeat Berkeley's question,

[27] Second letter to Berkeley, *Works*, vol. 2, p. 290.
[28] *Ibid.*
[29] *Philosophical Commentaries*, 14.

"does the perception of white differ from white?" If an idea and its perception are held to be identical, and the mind is thought of not as a substance but as a system, a place for perception can be found within this system, but ideas will have to become "part of the mind." It was Berkeley's doctrine that the mind and its ideas are entirely distinct and heterogeneous. Behind some very curious entries in the Note Book lies, at least in part I think, a sense of the disruptive impact made on the mind by the identification of the *esse* of an idea with its being perceived.

The soul is the will properly speaking & as it is distinct from Ideas.

The Spirit the Active thing that which is Soul & God is the Will alone . . .[30]

One wants if possible a unified Berkeley. The primary aim of this paper is to draw attention to the need for harmonizing interpretations of statements which are fundamental in his philosophy.

[30] *Philosophical Commentaries*, 478a, 712; cf. 708, 814, 847.

BERKELEY'S TWO CONCEPTS OF MIND*

C. M. Turbayne

Very little attention has been given to Berkeley's doctrine of mind either by Berkeley himself or by his critics. This is strange, because mind is the central concept in his system. He planned a book on the subject. It was to have been Part II of his *Principles*. In his notebook he wrote: "In Book 2 I shall at large show the difference there is betwixt the Soul and Body." He began this book, but then, as he said later, "I had made a considerable progress in it, but the manuscript was lost about fourteen years ago during my travels in Italy, and I never had leisure since to do so disagreeable a thing as writing twice on the same subject." He published Part I of the *Principles* in 1710, then, because of its poor reception, rewrote it in dialogue form. These books, however, are merely summaries of his whole project. He had planned Parts II, III, and IV to deal with mind, physics, and mathematics respectively. None was written, but *De Motu* (1721) and *The Analyst* (1734) are substitutes for Parts III and IV. He never produced a substitute for Part II. Why? Was it lack of leisure?

Berkeley's account of the mind is disappointingly brief. The mind is "a thing entirely distinct" from ideas. It is a substance in which ideas exist. Ideas are passive. Mind alone is active. The word "mind" does "not denote any one of my ideas," but I have "some notion" of the mind and its operations such as willing and loving, that is, "I understand the meaning of those words." I am immediately aware of my own mind, but I have only mediate knowledge of others. Here Berkeley's account peters out. He says nothing more about the relation between mind and body and nothing about memory.

But this concept of mind is inconsistent with the rest of Berkeley's system. He should have suffered the gravest embarrassment in retaining mental substance, although it is unperceivable, and in rejecting material substance, because it is unperceivable: mind, like matter, is nothing but an abstract idea.

* This paper is a synthesis of two papers appearing in *Philosophy and Phenomenological Research*, 20, 1 (1959): 85–92; and 22, 3 (1962): 383–386. Reprinted by permission of the author and the editors.

There is, however, latent in Berkeley's system, when correctly interpreted, another concept of mind. Had Berkeley developed it in Part II of his *Principles*, he would have avoided the inconsistency just described. But he would have suffered embarrassment of another kind. My problem is: How can I discover his *real* view of the nature of mind, given that his only systematic treatment of it is lost?

My point of departure is Berkeley's early note: "To behold the deformity of error we need only undress it." In his analysis of the errors committed by "the philosophers" Berkeley had the conception of "levels of error" or "layers of deformity" such that when any "deformity" was "undressed" another could usually be found beneath it. At each level Berkeley provides a diagnosis of a set of doctrines or attitudes held either explicitly or implicitly by philosophers. He indicates what their consequences or symptoms will be in the minds of plain men. Then he traces their causes through levels of delusion to their ultimate source. In this analysis-in-depth, four main levels are clearly distinguishable.

At the *first* level are the consequences or symptoms, noticed by Berkeley as skepticism, atheism, and vice.

These consequences "spring from" the official doctrine of the philosophers which, in Berkeley's diagnosis, is materialism. Materialism occurs at the *second* level of error. It contains three main doctrines. Two of these at least, by the time Berkeley wrote, had already stiffened into dogmas. The first I name "the dogma of the two worlds." This may be described as the doctrine according to which the everyday world is merely a representation of the real world of physical objects that science investigates. This doctrine leads inevitably to skepticism. The second doctrine I call "Hylopsychism," because it involves the supposition that personal characteristics such as forces or causes or active powers reside in physical objects. In Berkeley's analysis this supposition leads by psychological transition to atheism. For the third doctrine, whose essence is the inadvertent ascription of physical properties to the mind, I have coined the title, "Psychohylism." In particular Berkeley noticed that, although the philosophers regarded the mind as immaterial, they subscribed, nevertheless, to a doctrine of the embodied self.

In exposing the errors present in the official doctrine Berkeley reveals that the three dogmas depend, although not quite "at bottom," on corresponding errors at the *third* level. These errors are the fallacy of abstract ideas and certain fallacies of composition or category mistakes.

The delusions present in the doctrine of abstract ideas and in the categorical errors are rooted in errors in our use of language. Two fallacies occur at this *fourth* and deepest level of error. They are the ultimate source of all "the inextricable puzzling absurdities" that philosophers commit. They are:

(i) Treating general nouns as proper names.

(ii) Treating metaphors literally.

These two fallacies define the phrase "the mist or veil of words" in Berkeley's unpublished remark, "The chief thing I do or pretend to do is only to remove the mist or veil of words. This has occasioned ignorance and confusion." How do these idols-in-chief of the market place cause that idol of the theater, psychohylism?

The first is the source of "that strange doctrine" of abstract ideas, a doctrine manifested in every subject treated by the philosophers. Words like "will," "force," and "action" are nouns. There is, therefore, a disposition to regard them as names of things. Accordingly, realists and conceptualists were deluded to think that they could make a "division of things truly inseparable" (*De Motu*, 47), and then could inspect or introspect respectively, such precise, naked, and discrete "things-in-themselves" as the will, force, and action. Then, on the analogy of persons who can act or will or do things, the philosophers ascribed action or power to the corporeal world and used it as a mechanical principle of explanation. But the power to act or to do things belongs only to persons. The view that mind is part of the physical causal scheme was thus difficult to escape.

The second has made us prone to commit what may be called "the fallacy of composition" (*De Motu*, 47). Berkeley noticed that the philosophers used the person language in physics: " 'Solicitation' and 'effort' or 'conation' (I may add from other passages, 'force,' 'cause,' 'action') belong properly to animate beings. When they are attributed to other things, they must be taken in a metaphorical sense" (*De Motu*, 3). He noticed also that they used the physical language in psychology: "But nothing seems more to have contributed towards engaging men in controversies and mistakes with regard to the nature and operations of the mind, than the being used to speak of those things in terms borrowed from sensible ideas. For example, the will is termed the 'motion' of the soul: this infuses the belief that the mind of man is as a ball in motion" (*Principles*, 144).

Berkeley correctly did not object to the use of metaphor by philosophers. "Common custom," he said, "hath authorized" it. What he did object to was ignorance of its use. We must be constantly aware that we deal in metaphor, not in literal truth: "Most part of the mental operations being signified by words borrowed from sensible things; as is plain in the terms 'comprehend,' 'reflect,' 'discourse,' etc., which being applied to the mind must not be taken in their gross original sense" (*Three Dialogues*, III).

Thus the use of words like "force" and "action" in physics, and "motion" and "in the mind" in psychology, is legitimate and, in the latter case, unavoidable. But in such matters it was the lot of Berkeley's precursors—as it has been the lot of many of his successors—not only to speak with the vulgar, but to think with it. Unaware that they were using metaphors, the metaphors then used them. They believed that real forces reside in bodies, that bodies can really act or do things (Locke even wondered whether they could think), that the human mind has the physical properties of location in space and size, or that it is like a box or a room containing furniture. Berkeley himself was largely able to extricate his thinking from the physical connotations of "in the mind"—his favorite metaphor. In forgetting that they spoke in metaphor the philosophers not only denuded the mind of its defining property, but ascribed to it properties of the corporeal world.

Three strands run through the levels of error. Skepticism arises from the two-worlds dogma which in turn depends on the doctrine of abstract ideas. This in turn depends on the linguistic error that every noun names a thing. The other two strands are intertwined which suggests that Berkeley's philosophy of science and his doctrine of mind should be considered together. Atheism and vice are traceable through hylopsychism and psychohylism to abstract ideas and categorical errors. But these have their roots in the literal use of metaphors. To invent a metaphor such as *attraction* is an achievement. It is also an achievement to "undress" a dead one and to indicate that it can at most be a "mathematical hypothesis" and not the name of an occult quality. In one manner of speaking Berkeley's philosophies of science and mind amount to the "undressing" of certain dead metaphors. Berkeley's brief treatment of metaphor does not forbid the use of models in our understanding of the mind. That models are useful and even necessary can be deduced from his account. We must merely be on guard against treating models of the mind as the mind. The Id, Ego, and Superego of

Freud are no better and no worse off in this regard than the Self-love, Benevolence, and Conscience of Bishop Butler.

Let us see what is the nature of the theory of mind that follows from the preceding destructive analysis. Berkeley made the following points in three important fields:

In physics, the philosophers used words such as "force," "attraction," and "velocity" as names for entities. In Berkeley's analysis, their supposed referents are occult qualities, but though they name nothing they are, nevertheless, of great use in reasoning as explanatory devices, that is, as mathematical hypotheses.

In psychology, the philosophers used words like "reason," "the will," "appetite," and "pure intellect" as names for "distinct" entities. Berkeley cannot himself "abstract and distinguish so many beings in the soul" (*Alciphron*, 7.18).

In theology, there are words used that look like names, such as "Grace," "the Trinity," "Substance," "Personality." But in Berkeley's view, if these are treated as names, their referents are abstract ideas, that is, no things. He adds, however, that we can "assent to a proposition" although its terms name nothing. Thus the doctrine of the Trinity can become for a man "a lively operative principle influencing his life and actions" (*Alciphron*, 7.8) on the analogy with force and velocity and $\sqrt{-1}$. All these symbols are "instruments to direct our practice" (*Alciphron*, 7.11). Men cannot find things lurking beneath the names "Trinity," "The Will," "time," etc., although they "believe, know, argue, and dispute" about them (*Alciphron*, 7.9).

According to Berkeley, then: (a) some words are *cashed* immediately in things; (b) some words, although *cashable* in things on demand, are like counters in gambling, not *cashed* immediately; (c) other words are not *cashable* at all in things. Their meaning lies not in objects, but in actions of an actor. "I may be puzzled to define or conceive a notion of freedom in general and abstract," but, "it is evident to me, in the gross and concrete, that I am a free agent" (*Alciphron*, 7.18). Berkeley is often treated as though he holds that all words are like those in (a). This was a stage that he climbed through in early life. Some critics have noticed that he holds (b). But his view about (c) has been ignored, and, in consequence, much of his doctrine (e.g., his philosophy of mathematics) has been misinterpreted.

Where do mental words fit in this scheme? Clearly the words "mind," "will," "understanding" cannot belong in the (a) and (b) categories on Berkeley's own showing. In other words the mind, the will, and the understanding cannot be things at all. The mind cannot be called a substance—a thing in which ideas inhere—in any literal sense. To say that these entities are things or substances is, accordingly, to speak in metaphor. To think that they are is to fall into the philosophers' traps about metaphors, proper names, abstract ideas, and category mistakes. To think that they are not is to think with the learned. Thus, that the mind is not a substance, that the expression "mental substance" denotes nothing, that to say that mind is a substance is to speak in metaphor, all this follows from Berkeley's destructive analysis-in-depth.

The question now is: Did Berkeley entertain this second concept of mind? I think that he did for the following reasons:

First, even in his official account of the mind he treats the will and the understanding, considered as faculties, as abstract ideas. But he is all for retaining the words "the will" and "the understanding" (*Principles*, 27).

Second, it is difficult to conceive that Berkeley with his acute logical sense failed to notice the inconsistency involved in holding his official theory of mind.

Third, to hold the second concept of mind in reserve, as it were, to be given to the world in *Principles*, Part II, would be typical of Berkeley the tactician. Could he not have retained mind as literally a substance in Part I just as he retained matter in his *Essay on Vision*, "because it was beside my purpose to examine and refute it" in a mere summary?

Fourth, the last few pages of Berkeley's private notebooks—the *Philosophical Commentaries*—suggest that he was approaching a different theory of mind: There is no need for "a thinking substance, something unknown" (637) "No thing at all that wills" (658); "The substance of Spirit we do not know, it not being knowable" (701); "There must be a disposition to act" (777); "Substance of a Spirit is that it acts, causes, wills, operates, or, if you please (to avoid the quibble that may be made on the word it), to act, cause, will, operate its substance is not knowable not being an Idea" (829); "I must not say the Will and Understanding are all one, but that they are both Abstract Ideas, i.e., none at all" (871). In addition to entries of this nature Berkeley writes that he must use the word "Mind" instead of "person," "lest offence be given" (713), and, two entries later, "N.B. to use utmost Caution not to give the least Handle of offence to the Church or Church-men" (715).

From these considerations I suggest that there is latent in Berkeley's writings another theory of mind whose elements are sketched independently of any motive of prudence. His official theory is a brilliant attempt to superadd elements compatible with Christian theology (notably the doctrine of the self as substance, soul, or spirit). The second secret doctrine merely hints at a theory of mind which is the inevitable conclusion of an argument that Berkeley has been following wherever it might lead, no matter how much "handle of offence to the Church or Church-men" it would, most assuredly, give.

In a recent paper[1] Mr. S. A. Grave has objected that I do not say what Berkeley's secret theory was. My labels "official" and "secret" were, perhaps, inappropriate, but they represent a distinction which is, I think, easy to grasp. Berkeley was interested in metaphor. As a philosopher of science he tried to show that contemporary physicists and psychologists were victimised by certain metaphors. As a scientist within the science of optics it can be argued that he practiced what he preached, for he showed how to use the language metaphor to set up a theory of vision.

When he came to present his own psychology, however, he gave the impression that he too was a victim, that he took the assertion "Mind is a substance" in a literal sense, that he thought the soul was actually a "*substance*" "*in*" which ideas "*inhere*" and which "*supports*" the ideas, etc., hence the expression "*in the mind.*" This account I called Berkeley's "official doctrine."

But let us suppose that he practiced in his psychology what he preached in his philosophy of science and had practiced in his optics. We get an account in which the substance metaphor is used to make a theory of mind. This is what I supposed. Insofar as I argued, in addition, that this was Berkeley's real view, I called it his "secret doctrine."

Mr. Grave objects, however, that if Berkeley held that to say "The mind is a substance" is to speak in metaphor, then he could not have regarded his "official theory" of the mind as a theory at all, but merely as a way of speaking. This is strange. I cannot see why, for example, Plato and Berkeley must regard their theories of man and vision as not really theories but merely ways of speaking even though they regard the assertions "Man is a state" and "Vision is a language" as metaphorical. Nor can I see why Berkeley cannot hold both that "we speak of spirits in a figurative style" (*Alciphron*, 7.13) and that we make our theories of spirits from such figures.

Mr. Grave says that I really argued for the view that Berkeley had a "purely anti-substantivalist conception" of the mind which he expressed literally in private (the mind is not a substance) and meta-phorically in public (the mind is a substance). This is a peculiar correction. He would have been nearer the mark if he had said that I argued that Berkeley had a "purely substantivalist conception" of the mind confirmed by his private utterances. If I had argued that Churchill was using the phrase "the iron curtain" metaphorically, and then had had the good fortune to find him saying in his memoirs, posthumously published, that he thought the Russian boundary was really neither a curtain nor made of iron, my view would have been not a little confirmed. I should then have been inclined to say not that Sir Winston held an "anti-iron curtain" concept but rather an "iron curtain" concept of the Russian boundary. I did argue, however, that Berkeley was speaking metaphorically when he said "The mind is a substance." In which case the passages that I (and, happily, Mr. Grave) quoted from Berkeley's posthumously published private note-book to the effect that the mind is *not* a substance confirm my view.

Finally, Mr. Grave rejects my theory because of its "moral improbability": We have "what amounts to Berkeley's word for it that he did adopt the substantivalist concept." In other words, if Berke-ley believed that mind is not a substance and said it was, then he was a liar: We must take Berkeley literally when he said that the mind is a substance because he said that the mind is a substance. Now it is true that Berkeley adopted the substance conception of mind just as he adopted the language conception of vision, but this does not mean that we must take him literally, and if not, that he was a liar. Although most metaphors come unlabeled, their users need tell no lies. Churchill did not say: Mussolini is a utensil, metaphorically speaking," but he did say that Mussolini was a utensil, metaphorically speaking, and what he said was no lie.

While I cannot be sure that Berkeley had the awareness I ascribe to him, there are two factors which I think Mr. Grave has ignored. The *first* is this. Among philosophers Berkeley is notorious for his sharp distinction between speaking strictly or literally and speaking metaphorically, and for pressing this distinction further than most. "Speech is metaphorical more than we imagine" (*Commentaries*, 175). We speak strictly or literally when we attribute energy, effort, force, action to persons, for "they belong properly to animate beings." But (astonishingly enough from our prejudiced point of view) "when they are attributed to other things, they must be taken in a metaphorical sense" (*De Motu*, 3). Such attribution is metaphorical because it "transfers the principle of action from the human soul to things outward and foreign" (*Alciphron*, 7.16), that is, it represents the facts about bodies in the idioms appropriate to souls or minds. Now the physicists did attribute force, action, etc., to bodies. Berkeley said to them: You suppose bodies in a literal sense to be forceful, active, energetic, and powerful. Thus, from his point of view, they took metaphors literally. Again, according to Berkeley, we speak literally when we attribute motion to bodies, and metaphorically when we attribute it to the mind. The psychologists fell into the same trap as the physicists. Berkeley said to them: "You suppose the mind in a literal sense to be moved and its volitions to be mere motions" (*Alciphron*, 7.16). Thus they too were victims. Were the physicists and psychologists to give up their theories because they involved metaphor? Certainly not, if they worked. Let these scientists merely become aware that they dealt in metaphor, not in literal truth. Let them retain their metaphors as "instruments to direct action" or as "operative principles." Nevertheless, from Berkeley's point of view, they did not choose the best metaphors.

The *second* is this. A man discloses that he is using a metaphor if he spells out both its literal and its metaphorical meanings. Let me illustrate. If Sir Winston Churchill, confronted with a recalcitrant audience in Fulton, Missouri, and forced to explicate what he meant by "iron curtain," had replied: "It is evident that 'iron' cannot here be taken in its usual or literal sense—as when we say that bars are made of iron; nevertheless, I know what I mean when I affirm that there is an iron curtain or screen between the East and the West, that is that the boundary between the East and the West is impenetrable"; he would have disclosed that he was using "iron curtain" metaphorically. In similar fashion Berkeley first gave the literal meaning of "substance" or "substratum that supports": "It is evident 'support' cannot here be taken in its usual or literal sense—as when we say that pillars support a building" (*Principles*, 16). Then, confronted with a recalcitrant audience, he gave the metaphorical meaning: "I know what I mean when I affirm that there is a spiritual substance or support of ideas, that is, that a spirit knows and perceives ideas" (*Three Dialogues*, III). But when, just a few pages later, he gave the same type of analysis for that auxiliary metaphor of "substance," namely, "ideas exist in the mind": first, "the gross literal sense—as when bodies are said to exist in a place," and then his vain attempt to say what he really meant, that is, to give the metaphorical meaning: "My meaning is only that the mind comprehends or perceives them." I say "vain attempt" because, ten lines later, we learn that "comprehend" is also a metaphor, and not a good one in its present context because it suggests the mind active. Whereas mind as "sub-stance" or "under-standing"—the passive container and support of ideas = the passive perceiver of ideas, demands a "passive," not an "active" metaphor. He was saying in effect: "The mind is passively active in perception."

From these considerations, in spite of Mr. Grave's valued objections, it still seems likely to me that Berkeley was looking for the best possible metaphors to illustrate the mind. "Sub-stance" with all of its associated idioms would have met many of his tests.

BERKELEY ON "ABSTRACT IDEAS"*

Monroe C. Beardsley

I

There are three propositions which I hope to demonstrate by the present argument. I contend (in Section II) that Berkeley's attack on abstract ideas is not made wholly compatible with his atomistic sensationalism; (in Section III) that Berkeley does not provide or employ a single definite criterion for determining the limit of abstraction; and (Section IV) that the doctrine of abstract ideas furnishes no real support to Berkeley's argument against the existence of material substance independent of perception. By "the doctrine of abstract ideas" I mean "the theory that there are no abstract ideas". But what sort of an idea would be an "abstract idea"? It would be one which "we are told"[1] by its defenders is achieved by abstraction; therefore it is this process which we must first consider.

Abstraction begins with an experienced thing (that is, a collection of qualities or ideas), and the first step (i) of the process occurs when the mind makes one quality the object of special attention. If a particular thing T consists of qualities Q_1, Q_2, Q_3, we can, Berkeley holds, "distinguish" and "consider" only Q_1 and ignore the other qualities of T, though they are co-present with Q_1 in our experience.[2] But he denies that we can perform the second step (ii), that of "resolving" T "into its simple, constituent parts, and viewing each by itself, exclusive of the rest".[3] If Q_1 could be thus "singled" out[4] and "framed" by the mind in separation from the other qualities, it would be an abstract idea. But such an idea does not occur as an element in consciousness. It is to be noted that in the second step the abstract idea would be

* From *Mind*, LII n.s. (1943), 157–170. Reprinted by permission of the author and the editor of *Mind*.

[1] *Principles*, Introduction, sec. 7.

[2] *Ibid.*, Intro., sec. 16.

[3] *Ibid.*, Intro., sec. 7.

[4] *Commonplace Book* 141; ed. G. A. Johnston (London, 1930); hereafter cited as *CPB*.

merely the original idea conceived in isolation; it would not be a *new* idea.

But we do not know precisely what the isolation must be in order that the idea may be truly abstract, and it is not easy to determine what Berkeley means by "exclusive of the rest". (*a*) If we understand these words literally, he *says* that the abstracted quality Q_1 cannot occur as an element in consciousness unless the qualities Q_2 and Q_3 also occur with it (for these are "the rest"). To give an example, if T has the qualities *square, red,* and *moving,* then this *square* cannot occur later in consciousness unless this *red* and this *moving* accompany it. But Berkeley obviously does not mean this, since he admits that we are capable of "variously compounding and dividing" our ideas, and this rule would prohibit the imagining of a centaur[5] or a "blue horse".[6] (*b*) We might interpret him to mean that Q_1 cannot occur later without being accompanied by any idea at all; yet this would be too trivial for his purpose. (*c*) The best interpretation I can suggest then is the following one. Berkeley seems to mean that whatever qualities (including Q_2 and Q_3) may be absent from a later thought of Q_1, we cannot think of Q_1 without at the same time thinking of such other ideas as will, with Q_1, constitute a complex idea of a particular thing. That is, if Q_1 is originally perceived as part of a thing (T), then it can only be conceived later as part of a thing. To say that there is no abstract idea of a particular *red* is to say that there is no idea of that *red* apart from a thing. We may then define in a preliminary way the abstract idea of Type A: it is a *particular* idea perceived as a quality of a thing and later (supposedly) conceived without any thing which it qualifies.

The second type of abstract idea requires (iii) a third step, by which[7] abstract ideas of Type A are themselves compared with each other, so that from a given class of abstract ideas we frame "a most abstract idea" which is not merely abstract, but also general. That is, given Q_a (the abstract *red*) and Q_b, Q_c, other abstract ideas, *blue, green, yellow,* etc., the mind frames an "abstract general idea", *colour,* which is not any particular colour, but is all and none of them. In this case there is a "twofold abstraction":[8] the particular colours are abstracted from particular objects, and then the general idea *colour* is abstracted from classes of the particular colours. It is to be noted that

[5] *Prin.,* Intro., sec. 10.
[6] *CPB* 766.
[7] *Prin.,* Intro., sec. 8.
[8] *Ibid.,* sec. 99.

the abstract ideas of Type B would be *new* ideas created by the mind; in the third step the mind does not merely select what is common to all particular colours, but forms an idea of *colour* that is not one of the simple ideas perceived as part of a given coloured object. In the case of T, *colour* is not a "constituent" idea (like *red* or *square*) that could be "considered" and later segregated; it could never be abstracted from things save by comparison of an idea abstracted from a thing with other abstract ideas. Therefore the formation of abstract general ideas of Type B would depend on and presuppose the prior formation of abstract ideas of Type A.

The abstract idea of Type B is still a simple idea, a quality; that of Type C is a complex idea of a "being", such as *man* or *humanity*. In this case "several co-existent qualities" of each thing[9] are abstracted (as in Type A), then each complex of qualities is compared with others (as in Type B), and another idea is formed which is in effect a complex of ideas of Type B, and like them is a *new* abstract general idea. Now it is, I think, fairly obvious that Berkeley's attack on abstract ideas is specifically directed against abstract *general* ideas (of Types B and C); at them Berkeley delivered his "killing blow".[10] For (*a*) they are the ones which are "contradictory"[11] and "inconsistent" (Locke's term), and (*b*) Berkeley regarded his theory of signs as supplying all that was required of these abstract general ideas, namely, a theory of the manner in which particular ideas can become general. But he saw that ideas of Types B and C are formed upon the prior step (ii), which yields ideas of Type A; and when he came to examine the ideas of Type A he rejected them as well. He rejected them, not because our ability to frame ideas of Type A implies our ability to frame ideas of Types B and C (that is clearly not the case), but because the purpose to which he decided to put his critique of abstraction seemed to require that he reject the first type as well: At an earlier stage of thought[12] Berkeley had noted that " 'Tis one thing to abstract one concrete idea from another of a different kind, & another thing to abstract an idea from all particulars of the same kind", thus recognising the distinction between Type A and Types B and C. But in the *Principles* both are condemned.

Berkeley sometimes writes, in giving illustrations of abstract ideas,

[9] *Prin.*, Intro., sec. 9.
[10] *CPB* 699.
[11] *CPB* 566.
[12] *CPB* 499.

as though he meant that there are certain *abstract* ideas that cannot be abstracted from other *abstract* ideas, as when he says that the mind cannot "frame to itself by abstraction the idea of colour exclusive of extension".[13] But he is, of course, always referring to a particular *colour* (Q_1) and a particular *extension* (Q_2) in a particular thing, and saying that neither of these can become ideas of Type A. It is not that we cannot think of colour without thinking of extension, but that we cannot think of a particular *colour* without thinking of some particular *extension*. The doctrine of abstract ideas can then be expressed in this precise form: there are certain classes of ideas such that no member of one class can be thought of at a given time unless at least one member of the other class is thought of at the same time. To say that shape cannot be abstracted from colour is to say that if idea x is a member of C_s (the class of all particular shapes) and x occurs as an element of consciousness, then there will be some idea y such that y is a member of C_c (the class of all particular colours) and y accompanies x. The phrase "element of consciousness" is meant to include in its denotation thoughts of all sorts (images, concepts, ideas). For Berkeley would not merely hold that x could not be an image without y; he would say what he says of extension: "I do not find that I can perceive, imagine, or anywise frame in my mind such an abstract idea".[14]

II

With the above preliminaries we can approach the first question: that concerning the relation of the doctrine of abstract ideas to the general framework of Berkeley's epistemology. From this point on, when I speak of "abstract ideas" I shall be referring only to ideas of Type A. Those ideas become abstract when they are separated from things. But when we examine Berkeley's conception of what constitutes a thing, it becomes something of a problem to decide why these ideas should not be separable from things. Berkeley's view of perception does not seem to permit, much less necessitate, his doctrine of abstract ideas.

The difficulty may be stated thus. Berkeley's definition of the word "thing"—exclusive of spirits, which come under the most gen-

[13] *Prin.*, Intro., sec. 7.
[14] *Theory of Vision*, sec. 123.

eral range of "thing"[15]—is given in the first section of the *Principles* (Part I). My senses, he says, furnish me in their separate ways with various ideas, "and as several of these are observed to accompany each other, they come to be marked by one name, and so to be reputed as one *thing*".[16] A "sensible thing" is a "collection" or "congeries"[17] of ideas "blended or combined together".[18] When the ideas first appear to the mind they come through various senses, by various channels; they are distinct and *several*, for they are observed severally to go together, and they may be "apprehended by divers senses, or by the same sense at different times, or in different circumstances".[19] Then they are "united into one thing by the mind".[20] It is the mind which gives them a substantial unity, and a name, and the mind is led to do this, not by any intrinsic relation among the ideas, but by extrinsic spatial and temporal relations; men, says Berkeley, select those collections of ideas which are "observed, however, to have some connexion in nature, either with respect to co-existence or succession; all which they refer to one name, and consider as one thing".[21]

If this is a true account of the manner in which Q_1, Q_2, and Q_3 came to constitute T, then we may ask with some surprise why the mind cannot abstract Q_1. Why can there not be abstract ideas of Type A? If things are "*arbitrarily* put together by the mind",[22] they should perhaps be arbitrarily separable by the same mind; if the ideas originally entered the mind as separated and discrete, it is strange that the mind should so tightly have bound them together that they can never occur again in the mind as separated and discrete. There are two explanations of this phenomenon which might be urged on Berkeley's behalf. (1) It might be said that there is an intrinsic and necessary connection between ideas as they are perceived and that the mind is to some extent guided by insight into this connection, in learning about objects. Then certain sorts of abstraction would be impossible. But Berkeley holds that we cannot discover any necessary connection between our ideas;[23] their only connections are adventitious and

---

15 *Prin.*, sec. 89; *CPB* 653.
16 *Prin.*, sec. 1.
17 *Three Dialogues between Hylas and Philonous*, III.
18 *Prin.*, sec. 3.
19 *Three Dialogues*, III, p. 319.
20 *Ibid.*, III, p. 320, 324.
21 *Ibid.*, III, p. 319.
22 *Prin.*, sec. 12.
23 *Ibid.*, sec. 31; see also *CPB* 896.

external. We know, and need only know, relations of "co-existence and succession" in order to form things.[24] As for *a priori* principles— such as one asserting a necessary connection between colour and extension—these principles (since they would have to be expressed in abstract terms) would be particularly abhorrent to Berkeley's basic position. (2) It is true that in the case of some of the rejected abstract ideas Berkeley could say that these cannot be *abstract* ideas because they are not ideas at all. This is true of abstract general ideas like *colour* and *humanity*, as I have explained above. What is not perceived as one of the distinct qualities of T naturally cannot later be abstracted from T and conceived as a separate quality. In this way Berkeley can account for our inability to abstract *some* ideas, and if he were to apply this account to all ideas that cannot be abstracted, he would be adopting Hume's clearly-stated maxim, "all ideas which are different and separable". But it appears that, though Berkeley wavers on this point, he does not ultimately intend to maintain this general principle; and in certain crucial cases he does not apply it.

As an example we may take motion. Berkeley sometimes speaks as though a particular *motion* is an idea we acquire through sight, but an idea that is not abstractable from particular *extensions* and *shapes*.[25] Now Berkeley also says that every *motion* includes relation,[26] and relations are not ideas at all.[27] But whether a *motion* be "not one idea",[28] or "on 2d thoughts" a "simple idea",[29] Berkeley never definitely suggests that its unabstractability is a consequence of its not being an idea at all. But this is not the case with extension. First we must note Berkeley's statement that "the mind, 'tis true, can consider one thing without another; but then, considered asunder, they make not 2 ideas. Both together can make but one, as for instance colour & visible extension".[30] This seems to mean that in perception we cannot even *distinguish* or *discriminate* two ideas, *extension* and *colour*, as particular elements of a plane figure. Here Berkeley verges close upon Hume's position. For though we may, he holds, distinguish between two kinds of visible extension, the mathematical and the common,[31]

[24] *CPB* 752.
[25] *CPB* 877, 499; *Free-thinking in Mathematics,* sec. 20.
[26] *Prin.,* sec. 112.
[27] *Ibid.,* sec. 89.
[28] *CPB* 188.
[29] *CPB* 448.
[30] *CPB* 330.
[31] *CPB* 396.

the former may be defined as simply the co-existence of point-per-
ceptions;[32] and the latter[33] is not a visual idea at all, Berkeley says in
some places, for there is no "idea intromitted immediately and properly by sight save only light and colours".[34] Thus, in a particular
object T, the shape *square* is, on this hypothesis, not an idea at all: "in
a strict sense, I see nothing but light and colours".[35] Now if this is
Berkeley's position, then it would explain why colours and shapes, for
example, cannot be abstracted: because they are the same idea. But
Berkeley does not consistently adopt this standpoint; it is more in
accord with the general position of the first part of the *Principles*
when we find him referring to the *extension, colour,* and *motion* as
"simple, constituent parts" of a particular object,[36] or when we find
him speaking of " a certain colour, taste, smell, figure and consistence
having been observed to go together",[37] which could not occur if they
were not discriminable ideas. Finally, we may observe that if two
particular ideas are unabstractable because they are identical, then
neither can be "considered" in itself, and Berkeley's explanation of the
manner in which we come to make words and thoughts general presupposes our ability to consider the particular ideas which Berkeley
holds to be unabstractable. For these reasons I submit (*a*) that in both
the *Principles* and the *Dialogues* Berkeley regards the particular unabstractable ideas as *genuine* ideas, and (*b*) that he offers no explanation
of the impossibility of abstraction in these cases.

III

I have presented reasons for asserting that Berkeley's doctrine of
abstract ideas derives no justification from his theory of perception
and is even in contradiction with it. But even if we were to grant that
he is right in holding that there are some ideas which are not abstractable, we would still have to enquire how we may know *which* ones are
not abstractable. The obvious reply to this is an appeal (which
Berkeley often makes) to immediate experience; but since his whole
purpose (that of removing ancient prejudices about abstract ideas)

32 *CPB* 295, 437; 263, 485, 385; 384.
33 *CPB* 459.
34 *Theory of Vision,* sec. 130.
35 *Ibid.*
36 *Prin.,* Intro., sec. 7.
37 *Ibid.,* sec. 1.

presupposes that the common run of philosophers have misinterpreted their own experience, this appeal does not suffice. Berkeley must provide a principle by which abstractable ideas are distinguished from non-abstractable ones, and by which the difference between them is made clear. We may put the question in other words: if qualities cannot be conceived apart from things, how do we know which collections of ideas may be things? What defines the limit of abstraction?

To this question Berkeley has an answer, but it is not a univocal one. "I do not deny it [the mind] may abstract in a certain sense", says Euphranor,[38] "inasmuch as those things that can really exist, or be really perceived asunder, may be conceived asunder, or abstracted one from the other". One interpretation to which this passage lends itself is, I submit, the following. A person may abstract those, and only those, ideas which experience indicates to be separable in fact, or to belong to classes of ideas which are separable in fact. If I have perceived at least one particular *shape* without any sort of *motion* at all, then I may later conceive any particular *shape* without conceiving of any *motion* in it. Conversely, if every particular *motion* I have perceived has been accompanied by some *shape* (that of the thing moved), then I cannot abstractly conceive any particular *motion* without conceiving along with it some *shape*. This interpretation I shall call Principle A, defining it as follows: The ideas of Class C_1 are abstractable (in the sense of Type A) from the ideas of Class C_2 if and only if (i) there is an idea x such that x is a member of C_1, and x was perceived at time t, and (ii) there is no y such that y is a member of C_2, and y was perceived at time t, conjoined with x. To illustrate this Principle: it would imply that motions are not abstractable from shapes, but shapes are abstractable from motions; that colours and shapes are not abstractable from each other; and that, if I have perceived, for example, an electric light bulb apart from a socket, then I may conceive any electric light bulb apart from its socket. So far, Principle A seems to suit Berkeley's purpose and to represent his meaning faithfully.

But if it is closely examined, difficulties appear. "I can", says Berkeley,[39] "consider the hand, the eye, the nose; each by itself abstracted or separated from the rest of the body"; and he evidently expects us to be able to perform the same feat. Similarly, he says that

---

[38] *Alciphron*, VII, 5; *Works*, II, 328.
[39] *Prin.*, Intro., sec. 10.

he is able to conceive a human head without a body, a human trunk without limbs, and a rose's smell without a rose, though he has not, he implies, perceived the members of these pairs separately. For, he reports, "I may, indeed, divide in my thoughts, or conceive apart from each other, those things which perhaps I never perceived by sense so divided".[40] Therefore Principle A is really too narrow for Berkeley's purpose; it limits abstraction too much and leaves too little freedom for the imagination. Moreover, Principle A involves a relativity for which there is no room in Berkeley's system. It must be stated in terms of every individual person's own experience, which bounds his ability to conceive abstractly; and as far as Berkeley's own experience goes he can therefore never be certain (as he appears to be) that Locke and Hylas have never experienced any colour without extension or any motion without a thing that moves.

Therefore Principle A is not enough for Berkeley; and indeed there is another interpretation of the *Alciphron* passage which seems to represent Berkeley's intention more truly. The limit of abstraction, according to this principle, depends not on what actually has occurred in experience, but on what may *possibly* occur. That is, abstraction "extends only to the conceiving separately such objects as it is possible may really exist or be actually perceived asunder".[41] This principle is, of course, wider than Principle A, for it permits us to abstract what has not been perceived in separation but might be perceived in separation (such as the human nose or the human eye). We then may define Principle B as follows: The ideas of Class C_1 are abstractable from the ideas of Class C_2 if and only if it is *not impossible* that the following is true: (i) there is an idea x such that x is a member of C_1, and x is perceived at time t, and (ii) there is no y such that y is a member of C_2, and y is perceived at time t, conjoined with x.

The trouble with Principle B is that it does not help us to decide just what ideas are abstractable, and what not. For how are we to know which combinations of ideas (objects) are possible or impossible? Experience, Berkeley admits, reveals no such absolute necessities. The only way we know (if indeed we do know) that colours and shapes cannot *possibly* ever be perceived or exist in separation is by consulting our own minds and asking whether we can conceive them to be perceived or to exist separately. But if we decide whether they can be

---

[40] *Ibid.*, sec. 5.
[41] *Prin.*, Intro., sec. 5, 10.

conceived abstractly by determining whether they can exist separately, and then decide whether they can exist separately by determining whether we can conceive them to exist separately, and then decide whether we can conceive them to exist separately by determining whether we can conceive them separately, then our decision in any particular case is thoroughly circular. The only escape from this circularity would be to say that they cannot be conceived separately because they have not in fact existed in separation; but this makes Principle B equivalent to Principle A. And in the absence of this conversion of Principle B into Principle A, Principle B really is not an informative principle at all. But Principle A seems to be both doubtful and too narrow for Berkeley's argument.

IV

At various points in his refutation of realism Berkeley insists (*a*) that the prevalence of this erroneous belief among philosophers has chiefly been due to their uncritical assumption that we possess abstract (and abstract general) ideas, and (*b*) that the untenability of the belief is clearly exposed when we realise that we do not possess abstract ideas. There is no doubt that Berkeley regarded his doctrine of abstract ideas (as well as his doctrine of abstract general ideas, which I shall not discuss) as an essential ground of his immaterialism. So insistent is he on this point that we should expect the connection between his idealism and his doctrine of abstract ideas to be quite plain. There are, however, fatal obscurities in this connection, and the more seriously one considers them the more significance one discovers in Hume's position in the first and second parts of the *Treatise*, Book I.

The provoking situation we encounter in trying to trace this connection is that Berkeley turns out (even at the early stage of development represented in the *CPB*) to be employing the word "abstract" as a synonym for "non-existent" and "unworthy"; and when he caps an argument for idealism with a poke at abstraction, we readily discover, in some instances, that abstraction has nothing to do with the case. For example, he declares that the object T cannot exist apart from the sensation of it, for the reason that T cannot be abstracted from the sensation of it. But his statement[42] that "the object and the

---

[42] *Prin.*, sec. 5.

sensation are the same thing and cannot therefore be abstracted from each other" seems to mean only that T cannot be abstracted from Q_1, Q_2, and Q_3, since it is by definition just the combination of them. But since T is just its combined qualities (which are ideas), then T cannot even be *distinguished* from them (by step i), let alone *abstracted* from them (by step ii), so it is difficult to see how Berkeley's doctrine that there are ideas which are distinguishable but not abstractable (that is, which may be "considered" but not "separated") is relevant to the present case. Moreover, it may be a fact that "when we do our utmost to conceive the existence of external bodies, we are all the while only contemplating our own ideas",[43] but if we cannot do more than this, the important question arises: how did we come to think we could?

We seem to be opening a more fundamental vein of Berkeley's argument when we examine his statement that, "as it is impossible for me to see or feel anything without an actual sensation of that thing, so is it impossible for me to conceive in my thoughts any sensible thing or object distinct from the sensation or perception of it".[44] This assumes a shape different from that of the argument just considered, and at first seems clearly to turn on the doctrine of abstract ideas. We believe (*a*) that we can conceive a given object T as existing apart from the perception of it by someone; we make this mistake because we think on superficial examination (*b*) that we can have an idea of T existing without having any idea that T is being perceived. But the fact is (*c*) that we have never perceived T without perceiving it, and this fact (*c*), by Principle A, makes proposition (*b*) false. Our belief (*a*) is therefore ungrounded, and it follows from a denial of (*a*) that T cannot exist apart from our perception of it.

Now it is clear that the crucial point of this argument is the demonstration that the idea *T existing* cannot be abstracted from the idea *T being perceived*.[45] When we look about for Berkeley's demonstration, we discover that he very often says quite explicitly (1) that the reason is, that "the existence of an idea consists in being perceived";[46] that, in short, the ideas are the same.[47] To be precise, we must heed his warning: "But it must be well noted that existence is vulgarly restrain'd to actuall perception, & that I use the word existence

43 *Ibid.*, sec. 23.
44 *Prin.*, sec. 5; *Three Dialogues*, I, pp. 261–62.
45 *Prin.*, sec. 143.
46 *Ibid.*, sec. 2.
47 *Ibid.*, sec. 3; *CPB* 404.

in a larger sense than ordinary".[48] We can then express this view by the proposition that "T existing" is precisely identical in meaning to "T being thought of" in the widest sense (T_{ex} is T_{th}): "This I am sure", remarks Berkeley, "I have no idea of Existence, or annext to the word Existence".[49] That is, there is no unique idea of existence apart from perception: " 'Tis on the discovering of the nature & meaning & import of Existence that I chiefly insist".[50] According to this argument, then, "esse est percipi" is analytic; I have no *abstract* idea of T_{ex} for the same reason that I have no abstract idea of *colour:* it is not an idea at all.

Now this is a perfectly good argument, if it *is* Berkeley's argument. What is noteworthy about it is that it owes nothing to the doctrine of abstract ideas. T_{ex} is so far from being an abstract idea apart from T_{th} that it is the same idea; not only can it not be abstracted (by step ii) from T_{th}, but, being identical with T_{th}, it could not (by step i) even be "singled out" from T_{th}—indeed, it could not even be "distinguish'd therefore", as Berkeley admits.[51] If Berkeley's argument here is valid, then there could indeed be no "nicer strain of abstraction than to distinguish the existence of sensible objects from their being perceived, so as to conceive them existing unperceived".[52] Indeed one "might as easily divide a thing from itself", for that is precisely what one would be doing. But if the conclusion is that "to exist is to be perceived" is analytic, and for that reason true, it also follows that no one would even distinguish existence from perception, and therefore that no one could have been misled by the belief in abstract ideas to think that it is possible to conceive T_{ex} in abstraction from T_{th}.

As a matter of fact, Berkeley does not confine himself to the argument that "esse est percipi" is analytic; he also (2) holds to the position that it is synthetic. And this is quite incompatible with the other position, for in this case T_{ex} *is* an idea, distinct from T_{th}, but inseparable from it.[53] This argument does depend upon the doctrine of abstract ideas, as a statement of its steps discloses: (*a*) When T is perceived it is accompanied by the idea (T_{th}) that T is being thought of by some-

[48] *CPB* 472; 471.
[49] *CPB* 681; 680, 557.
[50] *CPB* 493.
[51] *CPB* 655.
[52] *Prin.*, sec. 5.
[53] *Ibid.*, sec. 6.

one; (*b*) no T has ever been perceived without being accompanied by such an idea; by (*c*) Principle A it follows that (*d*) T cannot later be conceived without T_{th}; therefore (*e*) T_{ex} (since it includes T) cannot be conceived without T_{th}, and hence (*f*) T cannot exist apart from being thought of.

We seem, then, to have discovered the point at which Berkeley applies his doctrine of abstract ideas to the refutation of realism. Step (*f*) of the above succinct version of his argument depends upon considering T_{ex} as an idea distinguishable, but not abstractable, from T_{th}. And yet it seems clear that Berkeley himself has provided his own answer to this argument. For we may ask whether steps (*d*) and (*e*) are in fact correct; "surely there is nothing easier than for me to imagine trees, for instance, in a park, or books existing in a closet, and nobody by to perceive them". To this Berkeley assents,[54] but he considers it irrelevant. It is no objection to his argument, he declares, to say that I can frame the idea of things existing "at the same time omitting to frame the idea of any one that may perceive them". This is only, he says, a case where "the mind, taking no notice of itself, is deluded to think it can and does conceive bodies existing unthought of, or without the mind, though at the same time they are apprehended by, or exist in, itself".[55] But (and this is the crucial question with respect to steps (*d*) and (*e*)) is not this possibility (which Berkeley here admits) that T_{ex} may occur in the absence of T_{th} (*i.e.*, that we may frame T_{ex} and omit to frame T_{th}) precisely what the doctrine of abstract ideas (as we have defined it in Section I above) denies? In the case of colour and shape, Berkeley strives to prove just this: that we cannot think of a colour without thinking of some shape. If we apply this to the present case, his argument must be that we cannot think of any particular thing without thinking that it is being thought of by someone. And yet in order to explain how philosophers have been tricked into realism by their belief in abstract ideas, Berkeley must (as in the passage above) contradict his general principle by saying that we can think of a particular thing without thinking that it is being thought of.

There is one more instance of Berkeley's use of the doctrine of abstraction which requires notice here. At one time he regarded the inseparability of the primary from the secondary qualities as "the great

54 *Prin.*, sec. 23.
55 *Ibid.*

argument"[56] against materialism. According to this view the erroneous belief that extension and motion can be abstract ideas apart from colours has been chiefly responsible for the error of realism;[57] and when it is realised that we cannot conceive extension apart from colour, it will be understood that extension cannot exist apart from colour; and since the latter is admittedly subjective, so also must the former be.[58] In view of all the preceding discussion this does not call for much comment. For if the proposition (*a*) that I have no abstract idea of extension apart from colour is offered as ground for the proposition (*b*) that extension cannot exist apart from colour, this inference can only be effected by Principle B, as discussed in Section III. But Principle B cannot be applied without either begging the question, or being converted into Principle A; and Principle A will not permit the inference of proposition (*b*), but only of the proposition (*c*) that I have never in fact experienced extension apart from colour. This is not to say that Berkeley's discussion of the relation between primary and secondary qualities amounts to no more than this; it is only to say that, as far as the doctrine of abstract ideas is concerned, the following conclusions seem to be warranted: (1) the doctrine appears to furnish less actual support to Berkeley's system than Berkeley supposes, and (2) it suffers from certain inner difficulties which cannot be removed without changing it in such a way that it furnishes no support at all.

[56] *CPB* 297.
[57] *CPB* 380.
[58] *Prin.*, sec. 10; *Three Dialogues*, I, p. 253.

PERCEPTION AND EXISTENCE

PHYSICAL OBJECTS AS PERMANENT
POSSIBILITIES OF SENSATION*

John Stuart Mill (1806–1878)

☆

We have seen Sir W. Hamilton[1] at work on the question of the reality of Matter, by the introspective method, and, as it seems, with little result. Let us now approach the same subject by the psychological. I proceed, therefore, to state the case of those who hold that the belief in an external world is not intuitive, but an acquired product.

This theory postulates the following psychological truths, all of which are proved by experience, and are not contested, though their force is seldom adequately felt, by Sir W. Hamilton and the other thinkers of the introspective school.

It postulates, first, that the human mind is capable of Expectation. In other words, that after having had actual sensations, we are capable of forming the conception of Possible sensations; sensations which we are not feeling at the present moment, but which we might feel, and should feel if certain conditions were present, the nature of which conditions we have, in many cases, learned by experience.

It postulates, secondly, the laws of the Association of Ideas. So far as we are here concerned, these laws are the following: 1st. Similar phenomena tend to be thought of together. 2d. Phenomena which have either been experienced or conceived in close contiguity to one another, tend to be thought of together. The contiguity is of two kinds; simultaneity, and immediate succession. Facts which have been experienced or thought of simultaneously, recall the thought of one another. Of facts which have been experienced or thought of in immediate succession, the antecedent, or the thought of it, recalls the thought of the consequent, but not conversely. 3d. Associations produced by contiguity become more certain and rapid by repetition. When two phenomena have been very often experienced in conjunc-

---

* From *An Examination of Sir William Hamilton's Philosophy* by John Stuart Mill (1865).
[1] A Scottish philosopher (1788–1856) who argued that the perception of independent objects rests on intuition, "direct deliverance of consciousness." (eds.).

tion, and have not, in any single instance, occurred separately either in experience or in thought, there is produced between them what has been called Inseparable, or less correctly, Indissoluble Association: by which is not meant that the association must inevitably last to the end of life—that no subsequent experience or process of thought can possibly avail to dissolve it; but only that as long as no such experience or process of thought has taken place, the association is irresistible; it is impossible for us to think the one thing disjoined from the other. 4th. When an association has acquired this character of inseparability— when the bond between the two ideas has been thus firmly riveted, not only does the idea called up by association become, in our consciousness, inseparable from the idea which suggested it, but the facts or phenomena answering to those ideas, come at last to seem inseparable in existence: things which we are unable to conceive apart, appear incapable of existing apart; and the belief we have in their coexistence, though really a product of experience, seems intuitive. Innumerable examples might be given of this law. One of the most familiar, as well as the most striking, is that of our acquired perceptions of sight. Even those who . . . consider the perception of distance by the eye as not acquired, but intuitive, admit that there are many perceptions of sight which, though instantaneous and unhesitating, are not intuitive. What we see is a very minute fragment of what we think we see. We see artificially that one thing is hard, another soft. We see artificially that one thing is hot, another cold. We see artificially that what we see is a book, or a stone, each of these being not merely an inference, but a heap of inferences, from the signs which we see, to things not visible.

Setting out from these premises, the Psychological Theory maintains, that there are associations naturally and even necessarily generated by the order of our sensations and of our reminiscences of sensation, which, supposing no intuition of an external world to have existed in consciousness, would inevitably generate the belief, and would cause it to be regarded as an intuition.

What is it we mean when we say that the object we perceive is external to us, and not a part of our own thoughts? We mean, that there is in our perceptions something which exists when we are not thinking of it; which existed before we had ever thought of it, and would exist if we were annihilated; and further, that there exist things which we never saw, touched, or otherwise perceived, and things which never have been perceived by man. This idea of something which is distinguished from our fleeting impressions by what, in

Kantian language, is called Perdurability; something which is fixed and the same, while our impressions vary; something which exists whether we are aware of it or not, and which is always square (or of some other given figure) whether it appears to us square or round, constitutes altogether our idea of external substance. Whoever can assign an origin to this complex conception, has accounted for what we mean by the belief in matter. Now, all this, according to the Psychological Theory, is but the form impressed by the known laws of association, upon the conception or notion, obtained by experience, of Contingent Sensations; by which are meant, sensations that are not in our present consciousness, and perhaps never were in our consciousness at all, but which, in virtue of the laws to which we have learned by experience that our sensations are subject, we know that we should have felt under given supposable circumstances, and under these same circumstances, might still feel.

I see a piece of white paper on a table. I go into another room, and though I have ceased to see it, I am persuaded that the paper is still there. I no longer have the sensations which it gave me; but I believe that when I again place myself in the circumstances in which I had those sensations, that is, when I go again into the room, I shall again have them; and further, that there has been no intervening moment at which this would not have been the case. Owing to this law of my mind, my conception of the world at any given instant consists, in only a small proportion, of present situations. Of these I may at the time have none at all, and they are in any case a most insignificant portion of the whole which I apprehend. The concept I form of the world existing at any moment, comprises, along with the sensations I am feeling, a countless variety of possibilities of sensation; namely, the whole of those which past observation tells me that I could, under any supposable circumstances, experience at this moment, together with an indefinite and illimitable multitude of others which though I do not know that I could, yet it is possible that I might, experience in circumstances not known to me. These various possibilities are the important thing to me in the world. My present sensations are generally of little importance, and are moreover fugitive: the possibilities, on the contrary, are permanent, which is the character that mainly distinguishes our idea of Substance or Matter from our notion of sensation. These possibilities, which are conditional certainties, need a special name to distinguish them from mere vague possibilities, which experience gives no warrant for reckoning upon. Now, as soon as a distinguishing name is given, though it be only to the same thing regarded in a different aspect, one of the most familiar experiences of our mental nature teaches us, that the different name comes to be considered as the name of a different thing.

There is another important peculiarity of these certified or guaranteed possibilities of sensation; namely, that they have reference, not to single sensations, but to sensations joined together in groups. When we think of anything as a material substance, or body, we either have had, or we think that on some given supposition we should have, not some *one* sensation, but a great and even an indefinite number and variety of sensations, generally belonging to different senses, but so linked together, that the presence of one announces the possible presence at the very same instant of any or all of the rest. In our mind, therefore, not only is this particular possibility of sensation invested with the quality of permanence when we are not actually feeling any of the sensations at all; but when we are feeling some of them, the remaining sensations of the group are conceived by us in the form of Present Possibilities, which might be realized at the very moment. And as this happens in turn to all of them, the group as a whole presents itself to the mind as permanent, in contrast not solely with the temporariness of my bodily presence, but also with the temporary character of each of the sensations composing the group; in other words, as a kind of permanent substratum, under a set of passing experiences or manifestations: which is another leading character of our idea of substance or matter, as distinguished from sensation.

Let us now take into consideration another of the general characters of our experience, namely, that in addition to fixed groups, we also recognize a fixed Order in our sensations; an Order of succession, which, when ascertained by observation, gives rise to the ideas of Cause and Effect, according to what I hold to be the true theory of that relation, and is in any case the source of all our knowledge *what* causes produce what effects. Now, of what nature is this fixed order among our sensations? It is a constancy of antecedence and sequence. But the constant antecedence and sequence do not generally exist between one actual sensation and another. Very few such sequences are presented to us by experience. In almost all the constant sequences which occur in Nature, the antecedence and consequence do not obtain between sensations, but between the groups we have been speaking about, of which a very small portion is actual sensation, the greater part being permanent possibilities of sensation, evidenced to us by a small and variable number of sensations actually present. Hence, our ideas of causation, power, activity, do not become connected in thought with our sensations as *actual* at all, save in the few physiological cases where these figure by themselves as the antecedents in some uniform sequence. Those ideas become connected, not with sensations, but with groups of possibilities of sensation. The sensations conceived do not, to our habitual thoughts, present themselves as sensations actually experienced, inasmuch as not only any one or any number of them may be supposed absent, but none of them need be present. We find that the modifications which are taking place more or less regularly in our possibilities of sensation, are mostly quite independent of our consciousness, and of our presence or absence. Whether we are asleep or awake, the fire goes out, and puts an end to one particular possibility of warmth and light. Whether we are present or absent, the corn ripens, and brings a new possibility of food. Hence we speedily think to learn of Nature as made up solely of these groups of possibilities, and the active force in Nature as manifested in the modification of some of these by others. The sensations, though the original foundation of the whole, come to be looked upon as a sort of accident depending on us, and the possibilities as much more real than the actual sensations, nay, as the very realities of which these are only the representations, appearances, or effects. When this state of mind has been arrived at, then, and from that time forward, we are never conscious of a present sensation without instantaneously referring it to some one of the groups of possibilities into which a sensation of that particular description enters; and if we do not yet know to what group to refer it, we at least feel an irresistible conviction that it must belong to some group or other; *i.e.*, that its presence proves the existence, here and now, of a great number and variety of possibilities of sensation, without which it would not have been. The whole set of sensations as possible, form a permanent background to any one or more of them that are, at a given moment, actual; and the possibilities are conceived as standing to the actual sensations in the relation of a cause to its effects, or of canvas to the figures painted on it, or of a root to the trunk, leaves, and flowers, or of a substratum to that which is spread over it, or, in transcendental language, of Matter to Form.

When this point has been reached, the permanent Possibilities in question have assumed such unlikeness of aspect, and such difference of position relatively to us, from any sensations, that it would be contrary to all we know of the constitution of human nature that they should not be conceived as, and believed to be, at least as different from sensations as sensations are from one another. Their groundwork in sensation is forgotten, and they are supposed to be something intrinsically distinct from it. We can withdraw ourselves from any of our (external) sensations, or we can be withdrawn from them by some other agency. But though the sensations cease, the possibilities remain in existence; they are independent of our will, our presence, and everything which belongs to us. We find, too, that they belong as much to other human or sentient beings as to ourselves. We find other people grounding their expectations and conduct upon the same permanent possibilities on which we ground ours. But we do not find them experiencing the same actual sensations. Other people do not have our sensations exactly when and as we have them: but they have our possibilities of sensation; whatever indicates a present possibility of sensations to ourselves, indicates a present possibility of similar sensations to them, except so far as their organs of sensation may vary from the type of ours. This puts the final seal to our conception of the groups of possibilities as the fundamental reality in Nature. The permanent possibilities are common to us and to our fellow-creatures; the actual sensations are not. That which other people become aware of when, and on the same grounds as I do, seems more real to me than that which they do not know of unless I tell them. The world of Possible Sensations succeeding one another according to laws, is as much in other beings as it is in me; it has therefore an existence outside me; it is an External World. . . .

Matter, then, may be defined, a Permanent Possibility of Sensation. If I am asked whether I believe in matter, I ask whether the questioner accepts this definition of it. If he does, I believe in matter: and so do all Berkeleians. In any other sense than this, I do not. But I affirm with confidence, that this conception of Matter includes the whole meaning attached to it by the common world, apart from philosophical, and sometimes from theological, theories. The reliance of mankind on the real existence of visible and tangible objects, means reliance on the reality and permanence of Possibilities of visual and tactual sensations, when no such sensations are actually experienced. We are warranted in believing that this is the meaning of Matter in the minds of many of its most esteemed metaphysical champions, though they themselves would not admit as much: for example, of Reid, Stewart, and Brown. For these three philosophers alleged that all mankind, including Berkeley and Hume, really believed in Matter, inasmuch as unless they did, they would not have turned aside to save themselves from running against a post. Now, all which this manœuver really proved is, that they believed in Permanent Possibilities of Sensation. We have therefore the sanction of these three eminent defenders of the existence of matter, for affirming, that to believe in Permanent Possibilities of Sensation *is* believing in Matter. It is hardly necessary, after such authorities, to mention Dr. Johnson, or any one else who resorts to the *argumentum baculinum* of knocking a stick against the ground. Sir W. Hamilton, a far subtler thinker than any of these, never reasons in this manner. He never supposes that a disbeliever in what he means by Matter, ought in consistency to act in any different mode from those who believe in it. He knew that the belief on which all the practical consequences depend, is the belief in Permanent Possibilities of Sensation, and that if nobody believed in a material universe in any other sense, life would go on exactly as it now does. He, however, did believe in more than this, but, I think, only because it had never occurred to him that mere Possibilities of Sensation could, to our artificialized consciousness, present the character of objectivity which, as we have now shown, they not only can, but unless the known laws of the human mind were suspended, must necessarily, present.

BERKELEY'S SENSATIONALISM AND
THE *ESSE EST PERCIPI*-PRINCIPLE*

Konrad Marc-Wogau (*Uppsala*)

A cornerstone in Berkeley's philosophy is his thesis of the infallibility of sense-perception. We meet it already in Berkeley's *Philosophical Commentaries* (=PC). One ought, he says, to trust the senses as people generally do. It is absurd to put aside the senses (entries 740, 539). In the published writings this idea is taken up with the same decisiveness. What "makes philosophy ridiculous in the eyes of the world" is that philosophers doubt of everything they see, hear, or feel (*A Treatise concerning the Principles of Human Knowledge* [=Pr.], § 88). And with a point directed against Cartesianism, Berkeley reiterates: "That what I see, hear, and feel does exist, . . . I no more doubt than I do of my own being" (*Pr.* § 40). "Away then with all that scepticism, all those ridiculous philosophical doubts. What a jest is it for a philosopher to question the existence of sensible things, till he has it proved to him from the veracity of God . . . I might as well doubt of my own being, as of the being of those things I actually see and feel" (*Three Dialogues between Hylas and Philonous* [=D.], *Works* of George Berkeley edited by Luce and Jessop, II 230). And he adds: "That a thing should be really perceived by my senses, and at the same time not really exist, is to me a plain contradiction".[1]

This assumption that the object of sense-perception necessarily is real or exists is a basic idea of sensationalism. Certainly, it would be wrong to call Berkeley sensationalist, if sensationalism means the doctrine that all knowledge consists in, or originates from, sense-perception. He assumes, as is well known, a special kind of knowledge which has nothing to do with sense-perception, viz. the knowledge of minds and relations. It is, however, possible to speak about the sensationalistic thesis in Berkeley's philosophy in respect to the above mentioned idea, that every sense-perception is a perception of something real. Berkeley, however, maintains a thesis of considerably wider

* From *Theoria*, XXIII, 1 (1957), 12–36. Reprinted by permission of the author and the editor of *Theoria*.
[1] Cf. *Prin.* Intro. sec. 22.

scope. The infallibility of sense-perception is due to the fact that perception is a direct awareness of the object, i.e. an awareness which does not imply any inference or associative transition from something to something else. Yet, according to Berkeley, all kind of perceiving, not only the perceiving of ideas of sense, has this nature of direct awareness. Also the perceiving of ideas of imagination and memory is direct awareness in this sense, and therefore free from mistake.[2] Thus the thesis that the perceived is undoubtedly real or exists is applicable not only to the objects of sense-experience, but to the objects of every kind of perceiving. I shall call this thesis the *extended sensationalistic thesis* in Berkeley, and shall express it as a formal implication:

$$(x) \ (x \text{ is perceived} \supset x \text{ exists}) \tag{1}$$

. . . Another basic thesis in Berkeley's philosophy is the *esse est percipi*-principle. It holds true of all ideas that their *esse* is their *percipi*. In *PC* this thesis is introduced as a new principle of great importance. "This I think wholly new. I am sure 'tis new to me", Berkeley writes in entry 491. And in his published books he repeatedly returns to the principle in question, and uses it as an important premiss in many argumentations.

Though this fundamental principle is referred to and commented in many contexts, it is very difficult to interpret its meaning. The comparison of different utterances gives the impression that Berkeley, without observing it, takes the principle sometimes in one, sometimes in another sense. My first problem is to distinguish some of the possible senses of the principle between which the interpreter has to choose. I ask first what *"esse"*, then what *"percipi"*, and lastly what *"est"* can mean in the phrase *"esse est percipi"*.

1. Berkeley translates the word *"esse"* sometimes by "being", but most often by "existence" (or "reality"). In *Pr.* § 6 he says that the "being" of the sensible things "is to be perceived or known". In § 3 and often elsewhere, in commenting the principle, he asks, on the other hand, what is meant "by the term exist when applied to sensible things". This different translation may correspond to a difference in respect to what Berkeley intends to say. It is well known that the term *"esse"* has been used in mediaeval philosophy both for *"essentia"* and *"existentia"*. If *"esse"* is taken in the former sense, the principle could

[2] Cf. *Three Dialogues*, II, p. 238.

be interpreted as a statement to the effect that the property to be perceived is essential to ideas or sensible things or is implied by their very being, i.e. that it belongs to the notion *idea* or *sensible thing*.[3] If, on the other hand, *"esse"* is taken in the latter sense, the principle must mean that the existence of ideas, which is a property not belonging to the notion *idea*, involves their being perceived. Between these two interpretations there exists a fundamental difference. According to the former the principle is an analytic statement the truth of which follows from Berkeley's definition of the terms "idea" and "sensible thing" as objects of perceiving. The principle means that the property of being perceived necessarily belongs to the idea, in virtue of this definition. According to the latter interpretation of *"esse"* the principle may be non-analytic. It only states that there is, in respect to ideas, an intimate relation between their property to exist and their property to be perceived, a relation which does not necessarily follow from the meaning of the word "idea".

Berkeley considered his *esse est percipi*-principle as a demonstrable principle. "Newton begs his principle, I demonstrate mine", he says in *PC*, entry 407. It could then be concluded that the principle is not meant as an analytic statement in the given sense. There seems to be stronger evidence for the interpretation of the principle as a statement the truth of which does not follow from the definition of the term "idea". But it is, of course, also possible that Berkeley, without observing it, gave his principle different senses in different contexts.

Some evidence for the interpretation of the principle as an analytic statement in the given sense can be found at the beginning of the first dialogue. It is worth while to examine Philonous' argumentation in these pages. Here the discussion turns about the meaning of the term "sensible thing"; Philonous introduces the definition: "sensible things are those only which are immediately perceived". He then demonstrates that only sensible qualities, like light, colour, shape, sound, etc., are sensible things. In spite of the fact that he nowhere makes an explicit statement to this effect, his conclusion seems to be that the property of a sensible quality to be immediately perceived follows from the definition of the term "sensible thing".[4] Thus the statement that the quality of being immediately perceived is indispensable to a sensible thing seems to be analytic. It must, however, be

[3] Cf. *Prin.*, sec. 25.
[4] *Prin.*, sec. 4. The last sentence may, perhaps, be considered as such a conclusion.

observed that this argumentation is based upon a wholly unwarranted transition from the definition of "sensible things" as those objects, "which *can* be perceived immediately by sense" to the definition: "sensible things are those only which *are* immediately perceived by sense" (II 174; italics mine). In this context Philonous really shifts from one definition to the other, Hylas not observing the trap. The two definitions are indeed entirely different: that a sensible thing must be actually perceived, follows from the latter, but not from the former. Not before the third dialogue (II 234) does Hylas quite legitimately raise the objection: "I grant the existence of a sensible thing consists in being perceivable but not in being actually perceived". But by this time Philonous is able to refer to earlier alleged reasons that an idea cannot exist without being actually perceived. Thus, while at the beginning of the first dialogue the *esse est percipi*-principle, viz. that ideas exist only when actually perceived, is introduced as an analytic statement the truth of which follows from the definition of "sensible thing", the argumentation which follows clearly shows that the principle is not meant as an analytic statement of this kind. Only the assumption that the principle is not an analytic statement makes it also explainable why Berkeley felt a need of its demonstration.

2. The terms *"percipi"* (to be perceived) and *"percipere"* (to perceive) Berkeley uses in a very wide sense. As has already been indicated "perceiving" means direct awareness of ideas, i.e. an apprehension which does neither contain nor presuppose any inference or transition from one mental act to another. It is the opposite to "reason" or demonstrative knowledge. As awareness of ideas, it is also opposite to the knowledge of minds and relations which, according to Berkeley, is a special kind of knowledge, introduced in the later editions of *Pr.* and *D.* as "notion". Perceiving seems to comprise both sensuous and unsensuous cognition, not only the apprehension of sensible things and of ideas of memory and imagination, but also a kind of unsensuous knowledge of what something is. Berkeley e.g. uses the expression "to perceive the table" not only in respect to the apprehension which I or other finite minds have of the table, but also to God's perception of the table though "His ideas are not convey'd to Him by sense, as ours are" (II 241). According to one of Berkeley's letters to S. Johnson, it is easy to think of the mind freed from the body as having ideas of colour without an eye and of sounds without an ear (II 282). In these cases the perception might be understood in analogy to what Berkeley says

about God's having the idea of pain. God does not suffer pain, but he knows "what pain is, even every sort of painful sensation" (II 240). His perceiving of ideas is a kind of knowledge of what they are.—In *PC* Berkeley's mode of expression is more differentiated. There he speaks about "being perceived, imagined, thought on". In his published writings the term "to perceive" is a comprehensive term for all these different kinds of apprehension. When the *esse est percipi*-principle is discussed, the different kinds of apprehension are only seldom enumerated. The expression in *Pr.* § 6 that the being of ideas "is to be perceived or known", is one of the few exceptions.

It has been maintained that Berkeley's term *"percipi"* does refer not only to the actual, but also to a possible awareness of an idea. *"Esse"* is also *"posse percipi".*[5] This interpretation can be supported by a clear utterance in § 3 of *Pr.*, where Berkeley says: "The table I write on, I say, exists, that is, I see and feel it; and if I were out of my study I should say it existed, meaning thereby that if I was in my study I might perceive it, or that some other spirit actually does perceive it". Thus the existence of the table means that it can be perceived, or that it is actually perceived by a mind.[6] According to the theory of creation, worked out by Philonous in the third dialogue, things partly have absolute existence, as far as they are (actually) perceived by God, partly "relative or hypothetical" existence, as far as they have been made accessible by God's creation to possible perception of finite minds. The creation consists in God's decision that "they should become perceptible to intelligent creatures, in that order and manner which he then established and we now call the laws of nature" (II 253). That the table in my study exists in this hypothetical sense thus means that it should be perceived by me or some other finite spirit, if I or he be in my study.—There exist, on the other hand, many clear utterances by Berkeley showing that *"percipi"* in the phrase *"esse est percipi"* does not refer to possible, but only to actual perceiving. When Hylas, in the third dialogue, grants that "the existence of a sensible thing consists in being perceivable, but not in being actually perceived", Philonous blames him with the words: "And what is perceivable but an idea? And can an idea exist without being actually perceived?" (II 234). In *Pr.* § 78 Berkeley says that ideas "exist only in a *mind* perceiving them; and this is true not only of the ideas we are

---

[5] Cf. A. A. Luce, *Berkeley's Immaterialism*, p. 61.
[6] Cf. *Prin.*, sec. 58.

acquainted with at present, but likewise of all possible ideas whatsoever". The existence of a possible idea thus seems to mean that it is
actually perceived by a mind. When I am out of my study, the table in
the study is, according to Berkeley, always actually perceived, at least
by God. If it exists, it is actually perceived. The counterfactual that I
should perceive it, if I were in my study, may be true, but is irrelevant
to the question of the existence of the table.

But how should then Berkeley's utterance in § 3 be explained? I
think that the interpretation of the existence of an unseen thing in
terms of possibility of perception is a residue from Berkeley's earlier
way of thinking. In *PC* we are faced with this doctrine. There it is
connected with Berkeley's opinion that bodies are powers in active
substances. In the entry 293a we read: "Bodies taken for Powers do
exist when not perceiv'd, but this existence is not actual. When I say a
power exists no more is meant than that if in the light I open my eyes
and look that way, I shall see it . . . etc." In entries 98 and 185a
Berkeley again maintains the existence of a tree in the park or of
colours in the dark in the sense that we should see the tree and the
colours if we walked in the park or if light illuminated the colours.
Later Berkeley abandoned this interesting idea. It has to be observed
that at this time Berkeley had not yet laid down the argument for the
existence of God, an argument which plays an important rôle in his
published writings. One premiss of this argument is that the existence
of material things presupposes their actual perception. This premiss
obviously contradicts the earlier idea that the existence of bodies or
colours means that they can be perceived.

3. The interpretation of *"est"* in the phrase *"esse est percipi"*
presents a rather difficult problem. Here it seems to me quite certain
that Berkeley, without being aware of it, takes the term in two different senses, a stronger and a weaker.

A. A usual expression in Berkeley's writings reads that the *esse* of
the ideas "consists" in their *percipi.* Thus Philonous asks at the
beginning of the first dialogue: "Does the reality of sensible things
consist in being perceived? or, is it something distinct from their being
perceived?" (II 175; cf. II 42 *et passim*). This expression seems to be
plausibly interpreted, if we say that the property to exist and the
property to be perceived are one and the same property. *Esse est
percipi* then states the identity of *esse* and *percipi.* In contradiction to
the common opinion that the term "to exist" designates one property
and the term "to be perceived" another property, the new principle

states that both terms designate the same property, viz. a relation to the perceiving mind.

In different contexts it may even seem as if the *esse est percipi* were introduced as a definition of the term "*esse*", either as a declaration of the sense in which Berkeley wants to use this term, or as a statement what sense the term has in common speech. Thus Berkeley says in *PC* that he does not "take away existence. I only declare the meaning of the Word so far as I can comprehend it" (entry 593). In the entry 604 he is persuaded that people would agree with him, if they "examine what they mean by the word existence" (cf. entry 408). The same opinion Berkeley stresses in *Pr.* when introducing his new principle: "I think an intuitive knowledge may be obtained of this, by any one that shall attend to what is meant by the term *exist* when applied to sensible things" (§ 3).

Many investigators into Berkeley's philosophy have proposed the interpretation of the *esse est percipi* as a definition, at least as one alternative.[7] Another possible interpretation of the *esse est percipi* is as an analytic statement the truth of which follows from the definition of the term "*esse*". Both interpretations seem, however, to contradict the abovementioned fact that Berkeley tries to demonstrate his principle. Indeed his text contains several arguments in which the principle is deduced from different premisses. Such arguments would be out of place, if the *esse est percipi* were intended as a definition or an analytic statement the truth of which follows from the definition of the term "*esse*".

There is at any rate much stronger evidence for the interpretation of the principle as a synthetic proposition which states the identity of *esse* and *percipi*. But here again the vagueness of Berkeley's text makes it impossible to know exactly, whether the relation between *esse* and *percipi* aimed at by him is the relation of identity or a weaker one, e.g. of strict or formal equivalence. . . . I select the weakest formulation of Berkeley's principle in the sense discussed so far:

$$(x) \ (x \text{ exists} \equiv x \text{ is perceived}) \qquad (2)$$

(where the values of x are restricted to ideas).

It may be observed that the extended sensationalistic thesis in

---

[7] Cf. I. Hedenius, *Sensationalism and Theology in Berkeley's Philosophy*, 1936, p. 45.

Berkeley's philosophy (our proposition (1)) follows logically from the *esse est percipi*, irrespective of the interpretation of the relation between *esse* and *percipi* as identity, strict equivalence, or formal equivalence. If the *esse est percipi* is to be interpreted as the formal equivalence (2), then it can be said to be a conjunction of the extended sensationalistic thesis (1) and the formal implication:

$$(x) \ (x \text{ exists} \supset x \text{ is perceived}) \tag{3}$$

In many contexts Berkeley adduces the *esse est percipi* as an argument for the sensationalistic thesis. Thus in *Pr.* § 88, when denying the possibility of doubting the "things which I actually perceive by sense", he says: "it being a manifest contradiction, that any sensible object should be immediately perceived by sight or touch, and at the same time have no existence in nature, since the very existence of an unthinking being consists in *being perceived*". Again, in the following argumentation of the third dialogue the sensationalistic thesis is taken as a consequence of the *esse est percipi*. Here Philonous wants to show that the *esse est percipi* corresponds to the view of commonsense. "Ask the gardener", he says, "why he thinks yonder cherry-tree exists in the garden, and he shall tell you, because he sees and feels it. . . . Ask him, why he thinks an orange-tree not to be there, and he shall tell you, because he does not perceive it" (II 234). Both answers, Berkeley seems to mean, are quite intelligible, if the gardener tacitly presupposes as a premiss the *esse est percipi*-principle. They are instances of the two implications constituting the principle: *a is perceived ⊃ a exists* and *a is not perceived ⊃ a does not exist* (or *a exists ⊃ a is perceived*).

B. Berkeley seems, however, to take his principle also in a weaker sense which may be expressed by the formal implication:

$$(x) \ (x \text{ exists} \supset x \text{ is perceived}) \tag{3}$$

(or, perhaps, by the corresponding strict implication). Both in *Pr.* and in *D.* the presentation of the *esse est percipi*-principle is followed by a long argumentation which is meant as a motivation of this principle. But it is quite obvious that, in case the argumentation proves anything, it must be the weaker proposition (3) and not the stronger (2). The main question here is, whether or not the idea "can exist without being perceived", and this is what Berkeley denies.

Sometimes one gets the impression that Berkeley himself oscillates between the two senses of the *esse est percipi*. Let us consider the following argumentation in *D.* (II 230): "(*a*) ideas cannot exist without the mind; (*b*) their existence therefore consists in being perceived; (*c*) when therefore they are actually perceived, there can be no doubt of their existence". The argumentation consists of three propositions, here called *a*, *b*, and *c*. The second proposition is introduced as a consequence of the first, and the third as a consequence of the second. This second proposition *b*, which is the *esse est percipi*-principle, thus acts the part of the conclusion in one, and the part of a premiss in the other argumentation. "Therefore" in *b* shows that *b* is meant to express that *b* follows from *a*. Now if this is to be the case the *esse est percipi*-principle must here be taken in the weaker sense (3). In this sense, but not in the stronger sense (2), the principle indeed follows from the statement that ideas cannot exist without the mind [i.e. (x) $(x$ exists $\supset x$ is within the mind)], and from the presupposed premiss that to be within the mind means to be perceived by the mind. But here the *esse est percipi* also acts the part of premiss in another argumentation, an argumentation of the same kind as the abovementioned in *Pr.* § 88. As in this paragraph, the principle must here have the stronger sense (2), if the argumentation shall be conclusive. If the passage quoted is really meant as an argumentation, it illustrates how the sense of the *esse est percipi*-principle can suddenly change in Berkeley's text.—Also another interpretation is of course possible: It could be said that the *esse est percipi*-principle always has the stronger sense (2), and that the argumentation quoted is logically inconclusive. The former interpretation is, however, preferable. The alternative, viz. that Berkeley did not clearly distinguish between the different senses of the term "*est*", is less improbable than the alternative that he has committed the more obvious logical fault which otherwise his argumentation would be found to contain.

Let us, however, drop the question, whether the weaker proposition (3) or the stronger proposition (2) expresses what Berkeley called the *esse est percipi*-principle. The essential point is that the proposition (3) has a great importance in Berkeley's philosophy, and that this proposition already expresses his idealism. (3) is also the proposition which Berkeley strives to prove by different arguments. In the rest of this paper I want to discuss one of these arguments. It is the argument which according to Berkeley is sufficient to prove his idealism. Berkeley is willing to abandon his idealistic philosophy, if the argument can be refuted. (Cf. *Pr.* § 22, *D.* II 200.)

The argument in question refers to what Perry has called "the ego-centric predicament", and is intended to prove our proposition (3). It is alluded to in *PC*, entry 472, and elaborated in *Pr.* § 23 and the first dialogue (II 200). In *Pr.* Berkeley asks, whether we could imagine trees in a park, or books in a closet, and nobody present to perceive them. His answer is that this can easily be done by framing in our minds certain ideas of trees and books, and at the same time omitting to frame an idea of anyone who may perceive them. But also then we ourselves must perceive them or think of them all the time. Although nobody is imagined to perceive the ideas, they are nevertheless perceived. But to imagine or to perceive ideas as not perceived at all is a contradiction. In order to show that ideas exist without the mind or unperceived, "it is necessary that you conceive them existing unconceived or unthought of, which is a manifest repugnancy".—In a similar way the argument is presented in the first dialogue. Hylas declares: "what more easy than to conceive a tree or house existing by itself independent of, and unperceived by any mind whatsoever?" Philonous then presses him: "How say you, Hylas, can you see a thing which is at the same time unseen? . . . Is it not as great a contradiction to talk of *conceiving* a thing which is *unconceived?* . . . The tree or house therefore which you think of, is conceived by you" and thus "in the mind". Hylas then finds out his mistake, and declares: "As I was thinking of a tree in a solitary place, where no one was present to see it, methought that was to conceive a tree as existing unperceived or unthought of, not considering that I myself conceived it all the while".

Now, what is the logical structure of this argument, and which are its premisses? Different interpretations are possible. In the following I intend to discuss five different interpretations.[8]

I. In his famous paper on the ego-centric predicament[9] R. B. Perry, without mentioning any particular philosopher, points to the opinion of idealists that idealism can be proved by an inductive inference. The following seems to be his way of reasoning. Let us examine different cases in which an idea can be said to exist, e.g. a book in the closet, or a tree in a park, etc. Then we shall find that all these cases, without exception, agree also in so far as the ideas in question are perceived (at least by the person who examines the cases). Now, by the method of agreement the conclusion is drawn from the examined

---

[8] Cf. A. N. Prior, "Berkeley in logical form", *Theoria*, XXI (1955).

[9] R. B. Perry, "The Ego-centric Predicament", *Journal of Philosophy*, VII, 1910.

cases—unjustly according to Perry—that all ideas are perceived. Or, to state it in a different way which better fits Berkeley's words: in order to show the falsehood of the statement that there exists an idea without being perceived, let us consider different ideas, e.g. a book in the closet, or a tree in the park, etc. When examining them we must still think of them; they are thus perceived. And this being the case in all examined cases, without exception, it is probable that there is no idea at all which exists unperceived. It is, however, very unlikely, that Berkeley in the passages quoted should have this argumentation in mind. Admittedly, he there considers different cases in which an idea is supposed to exist unperceived, and he shows that the idea is yet perceived, at least by the mind, who supposes it. But his conclusion seems not to be an inductive one. The issue is not that probably no idea exists unconceived, but that it is logically absurd to suppose an idea which exists unperceived. The exemplification indeed has its part to play, but rather as an illustration *in concreto* than as an induction. To prove the statement that every idea which exists is perceived, Berkeley endeavours to show the absurdity of supposing that there exists an unperceived idea. And in order to show this he discusses some examples. He argues as follows: it is absurd to suppose that the idea of a book exists unperceived, or that the idea of a tree exists unperceived, or that any idea whatsoever should exist unperceived. This is, however, not an induction.

In the following interpretations (II–V) of Berkeley's argumentation I shall presuppose that this argumentation is a deductive inference, and that Berkeley intended to show the assumption of an idea, which exists unperceived, to be not only false, but logically absurd.

II. According to this second interpretation it is absurd to suppose that an idea should exist unperceived, since this supposition itself entails that the idea in question is perceived. The argumentation looks like a *reductio ad absurdum* of the type $(\sim p \supset p) \supset p$. A proposition p (in our case the proposition *no idea exists unperceived*) is proved by showing that the negation of p implies p. I say that the argumentation "looks like" a *reductio ad absurdum*, because it clearly is not a *reductio ad absurdum* in the strict sense, though it may, at the outset, seem to be one. The proposition which is shown to be absurd is, indeed, not the negation of the proposition to be proved, i.e. it is not the proposition

(a) there is an idea, x, which exists unperceived,
but the proposition

(b) I suppose (perceive) that there is an idea, x, which exists unperceived.

In other words: what is absurd is not the supposed proposition that an idea, x, exists unperceived, but the very supposition of it.

Now, Berkeley was persuaded that the proposition (b) is absurd, and that it follows from (b) that the supposed idea x is perceived; but did he believe that his argumentation is a *reductio ad absurdum* in the strict sense? It is possible. The interpretation II states that Berkeley's argumentation is meant as a *reductio ad absurdum*, and that Berkeley thus commits a logical fault: he confounds the proposition (a) with the proposition (b). (In order to give a psychological explanation of this confusion, one could refer to the fact that if somebody utters "p" he expresses what he means, i.e. p, and usually also that he believes in or supposes p. This makes it easy to confound the supposition of p with p itself.)

III. Another interpretation is that Berkeley did not confuse the propositions (a) and (b). He found the transition from (a) to (b) quite natural and consistent, because he tacitly presupposed a premiss which makes the transition reasonable, e.g. the premiss that (a) implies (b). In this case his argumentation runs as follows. In order to prove the proposition (p) that no idea exists unperceived, let us suppose its negation ($=$a) to be true. Now, if (a) is true, also (b) is true (according to the tacitly presupposed premiss). But if (b) is true, it follows that x, which was assumed to exist unperceived, is perceived, i.e. that p is true. Thus from the negation of p follows the truth of p, which is absurd. But is there any evidence for this interpretation of Berkeley's argument? It is quite obvious that Descartes' well-known argument that the proposition *I think* is indubitable, serves as a model for Berkeley's argumentation in the entry 472 of *PC*. Descartes' argument can be made conclusive by adding a tacitly presupposed premiss, a proposition quite analogous to the premiss mentioned above, viz. the implication: *I do not think* implies *I think that I do not think*.[10] It is natural to presuppose the implication between a proposition p and the proposition *I think (suppose) that p* in the part of Descartes' system, where he decides to doubt of all propositions, and not to suppose any proposition to be true, before he had clearly conceived the proposition in question to be indubitable. By his resolution not to accept any

<hr/>

[10] Cf. Konrad Marc-Wogau, "Descartes' Zweifel und der Satz Cogito, ergo sum", (*Theoria*, XX, 1954).

proposition without first examining and doubting it, Descartes eliminates all propositions which are not objects of reflection. In this situation, if a proposition p is true, also the proposition *I think that p* must be true. The premiss that p implies *I think that p* is under such circumstances intelligible in Descartes. Although Berkeley quite certainly had Descartes' argument in mind, when writing the entry 472, there is no reason to suppose that he laid down a premiss of this kind. As we shall see in a moment, Berkeley means that (b) implies (a), but his text furnishes no evidence for the supposition that he should believe that (a) implies (b).

The interpretations II and III both maintain that Berkeley's argumentation is meant to be a *reductio ad absurdum*. In meaning this Berkeley, according to II, commits a logical fault; according to III his argumentation can be made conclusive by adding a tacitly implied premiss, the weak, but rather strange proposition: (*a*) *implies* (*b*), which otherwise does not play any part in Berkeley's philosophy. If we only had to choose between these two interpretations, the choice would be very difficult. The suggested supplementary premiss being rather far-fetched, I should recommend the interpretation II, in spite of the rule, proposed in the introduction, according to which an interpretation by introduction of tacitly presupposed premises is preferable to the view that the argument is a logical mistake. Fortunately there exist other possible interpretations (IV and V). According to them Berkeley's argument is not meant to be a *reductio ad absurdum* in a strict sense.

IV. The interpretation IV starts from the following idea. Berkeley may have meant the proposition *an idea, x, is perceived* to be such that it is absurd to question its truth, because the proposition *I suppose, that the proposition in question is false* entails that the proposition is true. The proposition *an idea, x, is perceived* is in this sense indubitable. Its truth follows from the supposition that it is false. According to the interpretation IV Berkeley may have been of the opinion that the questioning of a proposition p is absurd, and p itself indubitable, if p is such that its truth follows from the questioning of p (i.e. from the proposition *I suppose that p is false*). Some evidence for this interpretation may, perhaps, be found in *PC*, entry 472, which probably is the first outcast of the argument elaborated in *Pr.* and *D.*, although there are obvious differences. Berkeley here wants to prove that existence is necessary to an idea. The passage ending with the condensed sentence "you can at no time ask me whether they (the ideas) exist or no, but

by reason of that very question they must necessarily exist", I understand in the following way. Berkeley first shows that it is necessary for
the ideas to be perceived. Then he concludes, referring to the *esse est
percipi*-principle which is presupposed here in the sense that the existence of the idea consists in being perceived, that existence is necessary
to the idea (the idea "must necessarily exist"). But how does he show,
that it is necessary for the idea to be perceived? The idea is—he
means—necessarily perceived, because the questioning of its being
perceived (or its existence), i.e. the proposition *I suppose (perceive)
that the idea is not perceived* (or *does not exist*) implies the proposition that the idea is perceived, and thus exists. That the idea is
perceived or exists is thus indubitable in the sense that the truth of the
proposition *the idea is perceived* logically follows from the questioning
of this proposition. Analogically, Berkeley's argumentation in *Pr.* and
D. may be interpreted in this way: That the proposition *whichever
idea exists as perceived* follows from the questioning of this proposition, i.e. from the proposition (b): *I suppose that an idea, x, exists
unperceived*, proves, according to Berkeley, that the existing idea is
necessarily perceived.

A salient point in this argumentation as well as in II and III is the
supposition that the proposition *the idea is perceived* follows from the
proposition *I suppose that the idea is perceived*. If the interpretation
IV is correct, this logical relation (or, perhaps, the weaker one of
implication) between these two propositions must have been supposed
by Berkeley. Now, this supposition is by no means self-evident. We
have then to explain, how he could lay down this premiss. It has to be
kept in mind that Berkeley takes the term "perceiving" in a very wide
sense: it comprises different kinds of apprehension. In this connection
it is of special importance that according to Berkeley also a question
about something, a supposition, or even a mere mention of something
implies that this something is perceived. If I suppose that something, x,
has such and such qualities, I have perceived x. If an idea x is
mentioned, x is perceived, Berkeley holds forth in *PC*, entry 472. Start-
ing from this opinion about the nature of a supposition, Berkeley can
conclude that the proposition *I suppose that something, x, exists unperceived* implies that x is perceived, since to suppose something about
x implies to perceive x.

To sum up: According to our interpretation IV of Berkeley's
argument for his *esse est percipi*-principle Berkeley tacitly presupposes
in it two premisses. The first (a) means that a proposition p must be
considered as proved or necessarily true, if the truth of p follows from

the questioning of *p*, i.e. from the proposition *I suppose that p is false;* the second (β) means that to suppose something about *x* implies to perceive *x*. The former supposition seems to play some part in *PC*, entry 472; the latter follows immediately from Berkeley's definition of "perceiving".

If this interpretation is correct, Berkeley's argument may be criticized by questioning one of these premisses or both. An objection to the first premiss is this: In the case of a proposition which can be doubted, the truth of this proposition does not generally follow from our doubt. This is true, but it is not at all self-evident that a proposition must be considered as proved or indubitable, if its truth follows from the doubt of it. If Berkeley really has presupposed this premiss, the question arises, how he could take it as something self-evident or certain. We have then come back to the question, whether its explanation yet has to be found in a confusion of this situation with the one in which the truth of a proposition *p* follows from the negation of *p*. As an objection to the second premiss (β) one may insist upon that the supposition of something, *x*, having such and such qualities does not imply that x is immediately perceived, but only that *x* is pointed to by a description. If Berkeley's presupposed premisses are uncertain or not evident, his argument, of course, loses its force.

But there is another much more obvious objection against the interpretation IV. In the quoted passages of *Pr.* and *D.* Berkeley does not express himself exactly in the way supposed in the interpretation IV. He does not say that it follows from the supposition that an idea exists unperceived, that the idea is perceived. What he says is that it is a "manifest repugnancy" to perceive something as existing unperceived. He seems to understand the proposition *I perceive something, x, as existing unperceived* as a statement that *x* is both perceived and not perceived. He considers the proposition in question as absurd as the proposition *I see a thing which at the same time is not seen.* And this proposition is absurd, because it implies that the thing is both seen and unseen.

V. An interpretation of Berkeley's argument which seems to do better justice to this point is the following. A tacitly implied premiss is this: a proposition *p* must be considered as certain or proved, if the supposition of its negation, i.e. the proposition *I suppose that p is false,* is a contradiction. Now, with regard to the proposition *no ideas exist unperceived* it holds true, Berkeley may have meant, that the supposition of its negation, i.e. the proposition *I suppose that some idea, x, exists unperceived,* is contradictory, because it implies that *x* is both perceived and not perceived. Thus, the proposition *no ideas exist un-perceived* is proved.

The first premiss (a) of the interpretation IV is here substituted by a similar one (a_1): a proposition p is proved, if the proposition *I assume that p is false* is a contradiction. For this premiss there is, however, as far as I can see, no evidence in other passages of Berkeley's writings. It is not at all clear, why Berkeley supposes it here. The second premiss (β) of the interpretation IV is, of course, presupposed also in the interpretation V. But here also a third premiss (γ) is presupposed which is not at all self-evident, viz. that the proposition *I suppose that x is unperceived* implies that x is unperceived. This premiss must be presupposed, since the contradiction of the supposition of an unperceived idea consists, according to Berkeley, in the fact that this supposition implies that the idea is both perceived and unperceived. To this third premiss (γ) it may be objected that the expression "I perceive a thing as grey, though it actually is red" is common in ordinary speech, and that in certain situations it expresses a fact, and thus must make sense, and not be contradictory. For Berkeley, however, the statement that something is perceived with other qualities than it really has, is meaningless. If an idea, x, is perceived, x is exactly as it is perceived. This is, as pointed out above, one of the basic principles in Berkeley's philosophy, his extended sensationalistic principle. If this principle is accepted, the proposition that the idea x exists unperceived follows from the proposition *I perceive that x exists unperceived* and the proposition that x merely appears to me unperceived (though it really is perceived), must be rejected. The extended sensationalistic principle can thus be considered as a tacitly presupposed premiss of Berkeley's argument.

I have tried to give different interpretations of Berkeley's argument, and have in each case discussed the question, how his argumentation should be explained. The fifth interpretation which seems to me to be the most probable, as it most exactly follows Berkeley's words in *Pr.* and *D.*, states that the argument can be made consistent by adding three tacitly presupposed premisses. For some of these premisses some evidence can be found in Berkeley's text in other contexts. If they are presupposed, the statement becomes logically correct that the supposition of the existence of an unperceived idea is obviously repugnant.

It is reasonable to criticize Berkeley's argument by questioning these tacitly presupposed premisses. If they are dubious, the argument is not conclusive. But also a wholly different objection can be raised against it by examining its bearings on other theories in Berkeley's philosophy. Even if the argument can be made conclusive by supplementary premisses, it is impossible to overcome some difficulties or inconsistencies which the argument leads to in Berkeley's system. I shall conclude this essay by pointing at two difficulties of this kind which, as far as I can see, cannot be avoided by any reasonable explanation.

1. Berkeley's argument proves too little. What Berkeley wants to prove is that there can be no idea which is unperceived at any time. But from the proposition *I suppose (perceive) that an idea, x, exists unperceived* and from Berkeley's presupposed premisses it only follows that the idea is perceived at t_1, if the supposition is made at t_1, but not that the idea is perceived at any time. There is no contradiction in the supposition of an idea existing unperceived at all other times except the time, when the supposition is made. We must distinguish between two quite different situations: to perceive at a given time that an idea exists unperceived at that time, and to perceive at a given time that an idea exists unperceived at another time. If what happened yesterday (at t_1) is perceived now (at t_2), an idea which existed at t_1 is perceived at t_2; and this does not entail that the idea was perceived also at t_1. What the argument proves is thus not the whole thesis which is a cornerstone in Berkeley's philosophy.

2. Berkeley's argument proves too much. If it is conclusive, one of its consequences contradicts another wellknown thesis in Berkeley's theory. The argument implies that an idea about which I suppose something is perceived *by me*. But according to Berkeley's own theory an idea must not necessarily be perceived by me; it can exist as perceived by other minds, at least by God. From the argument, as interpreted above, it follows that it is impossible for me to suppose that an idea, e.g. the table in my study when I am out, exists unperceived by me, because my assumption of its existence implies that the idea is perceived by me. Berkeley's thesis that I can assume the existence of an idea unperceived by me, if only it is perceived by another mind, presupposes on the other hand that the supposition of something about an idea is possible without the idea being perceived by the person, who makes the supposition; and this contradicts one of the premisses of Berkeley's argument.

It has been maintained[11] that from the beginning Berkeley probably was of the opinion that I can only assume the existence of the

---

[11] Cf. Dawes Hicks, *Berkeley*, 1932, p. 113; A. Johnston, *The Development of Berkeley's Philosophy*, 1923, p. 190 ff.

idea which is perceived by me; only later he adopted the theory that the idea must be perceived by some mind, not necessarily by me who suppose its existence. If this is correct, it may be assumed that Berkeley let the earlier elaborated argument be a part of his theory, not observing that it now, by the change of his point of view, had become incompatible with other elements of the theory.

OF PERSONAL IDENTITY*

David Hume (1711–1776)

There are some philosophers, who imagine we are every moment intimately conscious of what we call our SELF; that we feel its existence and its continuance in existence; and are certain, beyond the evidence of a demonstration, both of its perfect identity and simplicity. The strongest sensation, the most violent passion, say they, instead of distracting us from this view, only fix it the more intensely, and make us consider their influence on *self* either by their pain or pleasure. To attempt a farther proof of this were to weaken its evidence; since no proof can be deriv'd from any fact, of which we are so intimately conscious; nor is there any thing, of which we can be certain, if we doubt of this.

Unluckily all these positive assertions are contrary to that very experience, which is pleaded for them, nor have we any idea of *self*, after the manner it is here explain'd. For from what impression cou'd this idea be deriv'd? This question 'tis impossible to answer without a manifest contradiction and absurdity; and yet 'tis a question, which must necessarily be answer'd, if we wou'd have the idea of self pass for clear and intelligible. It must be some one impression, that gives rise to every real idea. But self or person is not any one impression, but that to which our several impressions and ideas are suppos'd to have a reference. If any impression gives rise to the idea of self, that impression must continue invariably the same, thro' the whole course of our lives; since self is suppos'd to exist after that manner. But there is no impression constant and invariable. Pain and pleasure, grief and joy, passions and sensations succeed each other, and never all exist at the same time. It cannot, therefore, be from any of these impressions, or from any other, that the idea of self is deriv'd; and consequently there is no such idea.

But farther, what must become of all our particular perceptions upon this hypothesis? All these are different, and distinguishable, and

---

* From Hume: *A Treatise of Human Nature,* Book I, Part IV, Section VI (1739), and the Appendix (1740).

separable from each other, and may be separately consider'd, and may
exist separately, and have no need of any thing to support their existence. After what manner, therefore, do they belong to self; and how
are they connected with it? For my part, when I enter most intimately
into what I call *myself*, I always stumble on some particular perception
or other, of heat or cold, light or shade, love or hatred, pain or pleasure. I never can catch *myself* at any time without a perception, and
never can observe any thing but the perception. When my perceptions
are remov'd for any time, as by sound sleep; so long am I insensible of
myself, and may truly be said not to exist. And were all my perceptions remov'd by death, and cou'd I neither think, nor feel, nor see, nor
love, nor hate after the dissolution of my body, I shou'd be entirely
annihilated, nor do I conceive what is farther requisite to make me a
perfect non-entity. If any one upon serious and unprejudic'd reflexion,
thinks he has a different notion of *himself*, I must confess I can reason
no longer with him. All I can allow him is, that he may be in the right
as well as I, and that we are essentially different in this particular. He
may, perhaps, perceive something simple and continu'd, which he calls
himself; tho' I am certain there is no such principle in me.

But setting aside some metaphysicians of this kind, I may venture
to affirm of the rest of mankind, that they are nothing but a bundle or
collection of different perceptions, which succeed each other with an
inconceivable rapidity, and are in a perpetual flux and movement. Our
eyes cannot turn in their sockets without varying our perceptions. Our
thought is still more variable than our sight; and all our other senses
and faculties contribute to this change; nor is there any single power
of the soul, which remains unalterably the same, perhaps for one
moment. The mind is a kind of theatre, where several perceptions
successively make their appearance; pass, re-pass, glide away, and
mingle in an infinite variety of postures and situations. There is
properly no *simplicity* in it at one time, nor *identity* in different;
whatever natural propension we may have to imagine that simplicity
and identity. The comparison of the theatre must not mislead us. They
are the successive perceptions only, that constitute the mind; nor have
we the most distant notion of the place, where these scenes are represented, or of the materials, of which it is compos'd. . . .

We now proceed to explain the nature of *personal identity*,
which has become so great a question in philosophy, especially of late
years in *England*, where all the abstruser sciences are study'd with a
peculiar ardour and application. And here 'tis evident, the same

method of reasoning must be continu'd, which has so successfully explain'd the identity of plants, and animals, and ships, and houses, and of all the compounded and changeable productions either of art or nature. The identity, which we ascribe to the mind of man, is only a fictitious one, and of a like kind with that which we ascribe to vegetables and animal bodies. It cannot, therefore, have a different origin, but must proceed from a like operation of the imagination upon like objects.

But lest this argument shou'd not convince the reader; tho' in my opinion perfectly decisive; let him weigh the following reasoning, which is still closer and more immediate. 'Tis evident, that the identity, which we attribute to the human mind, however perfect we may imagine it to be, is not able to run the several different perceptions into one, and make them lose their characters of distinction and difference, which are essential to them. 'Tis still true, that every distinct perception, which enters into the composition of the mind, is a distinct existence, and is different, and distinguishable, and separable from every other perception, either contemporary or successive. But, as, notwithstanding this distinction and separability, we suppose the whole train of perceptions to be united by identity, a question naturally arises concerning this relation of identity; whether it be something that really binds our several perceptions together, or only associates their ideas in the imagination. That is, in other words, whether in pronouncing concerning the identity of a person, we observe some real bond among his perceptions, or only feel one among the ideas we form of them. This question we might easily decide, if we wou'd recollect what has been already prov'd at large, that the understanding never observes any real connexion among objects, and that even the union of cause and effect, when strictly examin'd, resolves itself into a customary association of ideas. For from thence it evidently follows, that identity is nothing really belonging to these different perceptions, and uniting them together; but is merely a quality, which we attribute to them, because of the union of their ideas in the imagination, when we reflect upon them. Now the only qualities, which can give ideas an union in the imagination, are these three relations above-mention'd.[1] These are the uniting principles in the ideal world, and without them every distinct object is separable by the mind, and may be separately consider'd, and appears not to have any more connexion with any

[1] Resemblance, Contiguity, and Causation.—Eds.

other object, than if disjoin'd by the greatest difference and remoteness. 'Tis, therefore, on some of these three relations of resemblance, contiguity and causation, that identity depends; and as the very essence of these relations consists in their producing an easy transition of ideas; it follows, that our notions of personal identity, proceed entirely from the smooth and uninterrupted progress of the thought along a train of connected ideas, according to the principles above-explain'd.

The only question, therefore, which remains, is, by what relations this uninterrupted progress of our thought is produc'd, when we consider the successive existence of a mind or thinking person. And here 'tis evident we must confine ourselves to resemblance and causation, and must drop contiguity, which has little or no influence in the present case.

To begin with *resemblance;* suppose we cou'd see clearly into the breast of another, and observe that succession of perceptions, which constitutes his mind or thinking principle, and suppose that he always preserves the memory of a considerable part of past perceptions; 'tis evident that nothing cou'd more contribute to the bestowing a relation on this succession amidst all its variations. For what is the memory but a faculty, by which we raise up the images of past perceptions? And as an image necessarily resembles its object, must not the frequent placing of these resembling perceptions in the chain of thought, convey the imagination more easily from one link to another, and make the whole seem like the continuance of one object? In this particular, then, the memory not only discovers the identity, but also contributes to its production, by producing the relation of resemblance among the perceptions. The case is the same whether we consider ourselves or others.

As to *causation;* we may observe, that the true idea of the human mind, is to consider it as a system of different perceptions or different existences, which are link'd together by the relation of cause and effect, and mutually produce, destroy, influence, and modify each other. Our impressions give rise to their correspondent ideas; and these ideas in their turn produce other impressions. One thought chaces another, and draws after it a third, by which it is expell'd in its turn. In this respect, I cannot compare the soul more properly to any thing than to a republic or commonwealth, in which the several members are united by the reciprocal ties of government and subordination, and give rise to other persons, who propagate the same republic in the incessant changes of its parts. And as the same individual republic may not only change its members, but also its laws and constitutions; in like manner the same person may vary his character and disposition, as well as his impressions and ideas, without losing his identity. Whatever changes he endures, his several parts are still connected by the relation of causation. And in this view our identity with regard to the passions serves to corroborate that with regard to the imagination, by the making our distant perceptions influence each other, and by giving us a present concern for our past or future pains or pleasures.

As memory alone acquaints us with the continuance and extent of this succession of perceptions, 'tis to be consider'd, upon that account chiefly, as the source of personal identity. Had we no memory, we never shou'd have any notion of causation, nor consequently of that chain of causes and effects, which constitute our self or person. But having once acquir'd this notion of causation from the memory, we can extend the same chain of causes, and consequently the identity of our persons beyond our memory, and can comprehend times, and circumstances, and actions, which we have entirely forgot, but suppose in general to have existed. For how few of our past actions are there, of which we have any memory? Who can tell me, for instance, what were his thoughts and actions on the first of *January* 1715, the 11th of *March* 1719, and the 3d of *August* 1733? Or will he affirm, because he has entirely forgot the incidents of these days, that the present self is not the same person with the self of that time; and by that means overturn all the most establish'd notions of personal identity? In this view, therefore, memory does not so much *produce* as *discover* personal identity, by shewing us the relation of cause and effect among our different perceptions. 'Twill be incumbent on those, who affirm that memory produces entirely our personal identity, to give a reason why we can thus extend our identity beyond our memory.

The whole of this doctrine leads us to a conclusion, which is of great importance in the present affair, *viz.* that all the nice and subtile questions concerning personal identity can never possibly be decided, and are to be regarded rather as grammatical than as philosophical difficulties. Identity depends on the relations of ideas; and these relations produce identity, by means of that easy transition they occasion. But as the relations, and the easiness of the transition may diminish by insensible degrees, we have no just standard, by which we can decide any dispute concerning the time, when they acquire or lose a title to the name of identity. All the disputes concerning the identity of connected objects are merely verbal, except so far as the relation of parts gives rise to some fiction or imaginary principle of union, as we have already observ'd.

What I have said concerning the first origin and uncertainty of our notion of identity, as apply'd to the human mind, may be extended with little or no variation to that of *simplicity*. An object, whose different co-existent parts are bound together by a close relation, operates upon the imagination after much the same manner as one perfectly simple and indivisible, and requires not a much greater stretch of thought in order to its conception. From this similarity of operation we attribute a simplicity to it, and feign a principle of union as the support of this simplicity, and the center of all the different parts and qualities of the object.

[The following is Hume's critical evaluation of his account of the belief in personal identity; it is from the Appendix to the *Treatise*.]

I had entertain'd some hopes, that however deficient our theory of the intellectual world might be, it wou'd be free from those contradictions, and absurdities, which seem to attend every explication, that human reason can give of the material world. But upon a more strict review of the section concerning *personal identity*, I find myself involv'd in such a labyrinth, that, I must confess, I neither know how to correct my former opinions, nor how to render them consistent. If this be not a good *general* reason for scepticism, 'tis at least a sufficient one (if I were not already abundantly supplied) for me to entertain a diffidence and modesty in all my decisions. I shall propose the arguments on both sides, beginning with those that induc'd me to deny the strict and proper identity and simplicity of a self or thinking being.

When we talk of *self* or *substance*, we must have an idea annex'd to these terms, otherwise they are altogether unintelligible. Every idea is deriv'd from preceding impressions; and we have no impression of self or substance, as something simple and individual. We have, therefore, no idea of them in that sense.

Whatever is distinct, is distinguishable; and whatever is distinguishable, is separable by the thought or imagination. All perceptions are distinct. They are, therefore, distinguishable, and separable, and may be conceiv'd as separately existent, and may exist separately, without any contradiction or absurdity.

When I view this table and that chimney, nothing is present to me but particular perceptions, which are of a like nature with all the other perceptions. This is the doctrine of philosophers. But this table, which is present to me, and that chimney, may and do exist separately. This is the doctrine of the vulgar, and implies no contradiction. There is no contradiction, therefore, in extending the same doctrine to all the perceptions.

In general, the following reasoning seems satisfactory. All ideas are borrow'd from preceding perceptions. Our ideas of objects, therefore, are deriv'd from that source. Consequently no proposition can be intelligible or consistent with regard to objects, which is not so with regard to perceptions. But 'tis intelligible and consistent to say, that objects exist distinct and independent, without any common *simple* substance or subject of inhesion. This proposition, therefore, can never be absurd with regard to perceptions.

When I turn my reflexion on *myself*, I never can perceive this *self* without some one or more perceptions; nor can I ever perceive any thing but the perceptions. 'Tis the composition of these, therefore, which forms the self.

We can conceive a thinking being to have either many or few perceptions. Suppose the mind to be reduc'd even below the life of an oyster. Suppose it to have only one perception, as of thirst or hunger. Consider it in that situation. Do you conceive any thing but merely that perception? Have you any notion of *self* or *substance*? If not, the addition of other perceptions can never give you that notion.

The annihilation, which some people suppose to follow upon death, and which entirely destroys this self, is nothing but an extinction of all particular perceptions; love and hatred, pain and pleasure, thought and sensation. These therefore must be the same with self; since the one cannot survive the other.

Is *self* the same with *substance*? If it be, how can that question have place, concerning the subsistence of self, under a change of substance? If they be distinct, what is the difference betwixt them? For my part, I have a notion of neither, when conceiv'd distinct from particular perceptions.

Philosophers begin to be reconcil'd to the principle, *that we have no idea of external substance, distinct from the ideas of particular qualities.* This must pave the way for a like principle with regard to the mind, *that we have no notion of it, distinct from the particular perceptions.*

So far I seem to be attended with sufficient evidence. But having thus loosen'd all our particular perceptions, when I proceed to explain the principle of connexion, which binds them together, and makes us attribute to them a real simplicity and identity; I am sensible, that my account is very defective, and that nothing but the seeming evidence of the precedent reasonings cou'd have induc'd me to receive it. If perceptions are distinct existences, they form a whole only by being connected together. But no connexions among distinct existences are ever discoverable by human understanding. We only *feel* a connexion or determination of the thought, to pass from one object to another. It follows, therefore, that the thought alone finds personal identity, when reflecting on the train of past perceptions, that compose a mind, the ideas of them are felt to be connected together, and naturally introduce each other. However extraordinary this conclusion may seem, it need not surprize us. Most philosophers seem inclin'd to think, that personal identity *arises* from consciousness; and consciousness is nothing but a reflected thought or perception. The present philosophy, therefore, has so far a promising aspect. But all my hopes vanish, when I come to explain the principles, that unite our successive perceptions in our thought or consciousness. I cannot discover any theory, which gives me satisfaction on this head.

In short there are two principles, which I cannot render consistent; nor is it in my power to renounce either of them, viz. *that all our distinct perceptions are distinct existences,* and *that the mind never perceives any real connexion among distinct existences.* Did our perceptions either inhere in something simple and individual, or did the mind perceive some real connexion among them, there wou'd be no difficulty in the case. For my part, I must plead the privilege of a sceptic, and confess, that this difficulty is too hard for my understanding. I pretend not, however, to pronounce it absolutely insuperable. Others, perhaps, or myself, upon more mature reflexions, may discover some hypothesis, that will reconcile those contradictions.

PHENOMENALISM*

R. M. Chisholm

1. Ernst Mach expressed *phenomenalism* by saying that "all bodies are but thought-symbols for complexes of sensations."[1] Where Mach uses "sensations" other phenomenalists may use "appearances" or "sense-data." And where Mach uses "thought-symbols," others may talk about language and "rules of translation."[2] But every form of phenomenalism involves the thesis that anything we know about material things may be expressed in statements referring solely to appearances. I shall now state my reasons for believing this thesis to be false.

2. It is true that whenever we perceive anything *x* to have some property *f* we have certain beliefs about the ways in which *x* appears. If a man now takes something to be a tree, he believes that, under the conditions now obtaining, he would *not* be appeared to in just the way he is appeared to unless the thing were a tree. And he believes that if he were now to act in certain ways—if he were to approach the thing he takes to be a tree, or if he were to reach out and touch it—he would be appeared to in still other ways characteristic of a tree. It is accurate to say, I think, that phenomenalism is based upon an interpretation of such facts as these.

The phenomenalist contends that, if we ask ourselves just what it is we are believing when we think we perceive something to have a certain characteristic, we will find that our beliefs really pertain only to the *appearances* of the thing we think we are perceiving. He then infers that our ordinary statements about physical things—such statements as "That is a tree" and "This thing is red"—*logically entail*

*From R. M. Chisholm, *Perceiving: A Philosophical Study*, Ithaca, N.Y.: Cornell University Press, 1957. © 1957 by Cornell University. Used by permission of Cornell University Press and the author.

[1] Ernst Mach, *The Analysis of Sensations* (Chicago, 1897), p. 22.

[2] Compare A. J. Ayer, *The Foundations of Empirical Knowledge:* "What is being claimed is simply that the propositions which are ordinarily expressed by sentences which refer to material things could also be expressed by sentences which referred exclusively to sense-data" (p. 232). C. I. Lewis has noted that the label "phenomenalism" is not altogether appropriate for the view here in question; see "Realism or Phenomenalism?" *Philosophical Review*, LXIV (1955), 233–247.

many statements referring solely to appearances. And he concludes that, if only we were to list the appearance statements entailed by any thing statement, we would have for that thing statement the type of translation the phenomenalistic thesis requires: we would have a set of appearance statements expressing everything that the thing statement is ordinarily used to express.

But is it true that such statements as "That is a tree" and "This thing is red" *entail* any statements referring solely to appearances—to ways of sensing? The familiar facts of "perceptual relativity" suggest that our ordinary thing statements do *not* entail any statements referring solely to appearances.[3]

Whether a material thing will ever present, say, a red appearance depends partly upon the nature of the thing and partly upon the conditions under which the thing is perceived. If one knew that the thing was red and that the lighting conditions were normal, one could predict that, to a normal observer, the thing would present a red appearance; if one knew that the lights were out, or that the perceiver had a certain kind of color blindness, one could predict that the thing would present some other appearance; and so on, for any other thing and its possible appearances. To calculate the appearances, it is necessary to know both the thing perceived and the observation conditions, for it is the thing perceived and the observation conditions working jointly which determine the way the thing is to appear.

The facts of perceptual relativity thus suggest that even the simple thing statement, "This thing is red," doesn't entail *any* statement about appearances; an appearance statement is entailed only when "This thing is red" is taken in conjunction with *another* thing statement referring to observation conditions. This may be seen further if we compare first the thing statement.

This is red (P)

and a categorical appearance statement

Redness will be sensed (R)

May we say, then, that the statement P above entails R, as these statements would ordinarily be interpreted? Possibly it is obvious that

---

[3] We should say, more exactly, that such thing statements entail no synthetic, or nonlogical, statements referring solely to appearances.

no contradiction is involved in affirming P and denying R. The following considerations, however, may make the matter clearer.

Taken in conjunction with certain *other* thing statements Q, referring to observation conditions, P does entail R. The following is such a statement Q:

This is perceived under normal conditions; and if this is red and is perceived under normal conditions, redness will be sensed. (Q)

(So far as our present point is concerned, it does not particularly matter how the expression "normal conditions" is defined.)

Taken in conjunction, not with Q, but with still *other* thing statements S, also referring to observation conditions, P entails not-R. An example of S would be:

This is perceived under conditions which are normal except for the presence of blue lights; and if this is red and is perceived under conditions which are normal except for the presence of blue lights, redness will not be sensed. (S)

As these statements would ordinarily be interpreted, S is logically consistent with P; there is no contradiction involved in affirming one and denying the other. But the conjunction of P and S, if it is logically consistent, must entail everything that P entails and cannot entail anything logically incompatible with what P entails. If P and S entail not-R, it is impossible that P entail R. Hence "This is red" (P) does not entail "Redness will be sensed" (R). Similarly, "Redness will not be sensed" is not sufficient to *falsify* "This is red." We may draw a similar conclusion with respect to any other categorical appearance statement R'. Although there may be a statement about observation conditions, Q', such that "This is red" (P) and Q' entail R', there is also a statement about observation conditions, S', such that P and S' entail not-R'; hence P does not entail R'.

According to some phenomenalists, the appearance statements entailed by statements describing a physical thing would be considerably more complicated than "Redness will be sensed;" they would be conjunctions of conditionals of the form "If such and such should be sensed, then such and such would be sensed." The phenomenalist might hold, for example, that the thing statement

There is really a door in front of me (P)

entails a conditional appearance statement of this sort:

If such-and-such visual appearances should be sensed (namely, those associated with reaching), then such-and-such tactual appearances would be sensed. (*R*)

Again, if *P* entails *R*, then it is logically impossible that there be a statement *S*, consistent with *P* and such that *P* and *S* entail not-*R*. Clearly there are many such statements *S*. If I am subject to systematic delusions, then one might be:

Whenever I see a door, I sense such-and-such visual appearances but not such-and-such tactual appearances.[4] (*S*)

This statement, in conjunction with *P*, entails not-*R*. Since *S* is consistent with *P*, it is false that *P* entails *R*.

By similar reasoning it would seem possible to formulate, for any complex appearance statement *R'* that might be thought to be an analytic consequence of *P*, some statement *S'* consistent with *P* and such that *P* and *S'* entail not-*R'*.

I believe we may say, therefore, that no synthetic thing statement *P* entails any appearance statement unless *P* is taken in conjunction with some *other* thing statement referring to observation conditions. In our earlier example, "This is red" (*P*) does entail an appearance statement when *P* is conjoined with *Q'* "This is perceived under normal conditions; and if this is red and is perceived under normal conditions redness will be sensed." And we have seen that, when conjoined with statements about different observation conditions, "This is red" may entail a different statement about appearances. Thus when John Stuart Mill tried to show, with respect to his belief that Calcutta exists, that it can be expressed phenomenalistically, in terms of "permanent possibilities of sensations," he specified these possibilities by reference to himself and to the banks of the Hooghly:

I believe that Calcutta exists, though I do not perceive it, and that it would still exist if every percipient inhabitant were suddenly to leave the place, or

[4] Compare C. I. Lewis's example in *An Analysis of Knowledge and Valuation*, pp. 248–249, where appearance statements are said to be "probability consequences" of thing statements. Whether Lewis's view is an instance of phenomenalism depends upon how *probability* is interpreted; see George Chatalian, "Probability: Inductive versus Deductive," *Philosophical Studies*, III (1952), 49–56, and Roderick Firth, "Radical Empiricism and Perceptual Relativity," *Philosophical Review*, LIX (1950), 164–183, 319–331.

be struck dead. But when I analyze the belief, all I find in it is, that were these events to take place, the Permanent Possibility of Sensation which I call Calcutta would still remain; that if I were suddenly transported to the banks of the Hooghly, I should still have the sensations which, if now present, would lead me to affirm that Calcutta exists here and now.[5]

But this method of deriving appearance statements from thing statements does not suggest any way of expressing "Calcutta exists" or "This thing is red" in terms referring solely to permanent possibilities of sensation, or to appearances. For we obtain our appearance statements only by referring to still other physical things.[6]

3. In "Radical Empiricism and Perceptual Relativity," which appeared in Vol. LIX of the *Philosophical Review* (1950), Roderick Firth proposed a way in which, he thought, the phenomenalist might meet such difficulties. The proposal was essentially this: such a sentence as "This is a doorknob" is in fact ambiguous; in *one* of its ordinary uses, Firth said, "This is a doorknob" *does* logically imply some such sentence as "If such-and-such appearances are sensed, there will be a feeling of hardness"; when the philosopher points out that there are conditions under which we would want to say that "This is a doorknob" is true and that the sentence about the feeling of hardness is false, then, according to Firth, the philosopher is appealing to some *other* use of "This is a doorknob." But this proposal has some very implausible consequences, as Firth conceded. One of these is the very supposition that "This is a doorknob" *has* such ambiguities, hitherto unnoticed by linguists and philologists or by carpenters and cabinet-makers. The other implausible consequence, more serious, is this: Let us suppose that, without realizing it, a man has acquired a disorder of such a sort that doorknobs cannot be made to feel hard to him. Firth's proposal implies that there is a sense of the sentence "This is a doorknob"—namely, the first one referred to above—which can be made false merely as a result of the man acquiring the disorder. To meet the difficulty posed by the fact of "perceptual relativity," Firth

[5] John Stuart Mill, *An Examination of Sir William Hamilton's Philosophy* (New York, 1884), p. 246. Compare H. H. Price's criticism of such theories in *Hume's Theory of the External World* (Oxford, 1940), pp. 183–188.

[6] In *Berkeley* (pp. 183–189), G. J. Warnock compares the relation between thing statements and appearance statements to that between the *verdict* a jury makes and the *evidence* to which the jury appeals. But any verdict that is just and reasonable is probable—more probable than not—in relation to its evidence. And I have suggested in Chapter Six that there is no statement about a material thing which is more probable than not in relation to any set of statements referring merely to appearance.

suggests, in effect, that the property of being a doorknob—in one supposed sense of the term "doorknob"—is *also* dependent upon the perceiving subject.

In "Two Dogmas of Empiricism,"[7] W. V. Quine described the thesis of phenomenalism, in its various forms, as being one of two untenable dogmas of traditional empiricism. Quine remained empiricist enough, however, to infer from the untenability of this dogma, not that empiricism is false, but that "in point of epistemological footing the physical objects and the gods differ only in degree and not in kind." Lewis, too, had argued that if phenomenalism is false then scepticism is true.[8] But it is only on the basis of still another "dogma of empiricism," left tacit in Quine's and Lewis's discussions, that one may regard the disjunction between phenomenalism and scepticism as being exhaustive or complete.

---

[7] W. V. Quine, "Two Dogmas of Empiricism," *Philosophical Review*, LX (1951).

[8] *See* C. I. Lewis, *An Analysis of Knowledge and Valuation*, Book I.

PHILOSOPHY AND SCIENCE

A NOTE ON BERKELEY AS PRECURSOR
OF MACH AND EINSTEIN*

Sir Karl R. Popper

The purpose of this note is to give a list of those ideas of Berkeley's in the field of the philosophy of physics which have a strikingly new look. They are mainly ideas which were rediscovered and reintroduced into the discussion of modern physics by Ernst Mach and Heinrich Hertz, and by a number of philosophers and physicists, some of them influenced by Mach, such as Bertrand Russell, Philip Frank, Richard von Mises, Moritz Schlick,[1] Werner Heisenberg and others.

I may say at once that I do not agree with most of these positivistic views. I admire Berkeley without agreeing with him. But criticism of Berkeley is not the purpose of this note, and will be confined to some very brief and incomplete remarks in section v.[2]

Berkeley wrote only one work, *De Motu*, devoted exclusively to the philosophy of physical science; but there are passages in many of his other works in which similar ideas and supplementary ones are represented.[3]

The core of Berkeley's ideas on the philosophy of science is in his *criticism of Newton's dynamics*. (Newton's mathematics were criticized by Berkeley in *The Analyst* and its two sequels.) Berkeley was

---

* From *Conjectures and Refutations* (Chapter 6), by Sir Karl R. Popper (New York: Basic Books, 1962, 2nd ed., 1965, Routledge & Kegan Paul Ltd.), © Karl R. Popper, 1962, Basic Books, Inc., Publishers, New York. Reprinted by permission of the author, Basic Books, Inc., and Routledge & Kegan Paul Ltd.
    [1] Schlick, under the influence of Wittgenstein, suggested an instrumentalist interpretation of universal laws which was practically equivalent to Berkeley's "mathematical hypotheses"; see *Naturwissenschaften*, 19, 1931, pp. 151 and 156. For further references see footnote 23 to section iv of ch. 3, above.
    [2] I have since developed these ideas more fully in ch. 3, above; especially section vi.
    [3] Apart from *DM* (= *De Motu*, 1721) I shall quote *TV* (= *Essay towards a New Theory of Vision*, 1709); *Pr* (= *Treatise concerning the Principles of Human Knowledge*, 1710); *HP* (= *Three Dialogues between Hylas and Philonous*, 1713); *Alc* (= *Alciphron*, 1732); *An* (= *The Analyst*, 1734); and *S* (= *Siris*, 1744). As far as I know, there does not exist an English translation of *DM* which succeeds in making clear what Berkeley meant to say; and the Editor of the latest edition of the *Works* even goes out of his way to belittle the significance of this highly original and in many ways unique essay.

90

full of admiration for Newton, and no doubt realized that there could have been no worthier object for his criticism.

The following twenty-one theses are not always expressed in Berkeley's terminology; their order is not connected with the order in which they appear in Berkeley's writings, or in which they might be presented in a systematic treatment of Berkeley's thought.

For a motto, I open my list with a quotation from Berkeley (*DM*, 29).

(1) *"To utter a word and mean nothing by it is unworthy of a philosopher."*

(2) The meaning of a word is the idea or the sense-quality with which it is associated (as its name). Thus the words "absolute space" and "absolute time" are without any empirical (or operational) meaning; Newton's doctrine of absolute space and absolute time must therefore be rejected as a physical theory. (Cf. *Pr*, 97, 99, 116; *DM*, 53, 55, 62; *AN*, 50, Qu. 8; *S*, 271: "Concerning absolute space, that phantom of the mechanical and geometrical philosophers, it may suffice to observe that it is neither perceived by our sense, nor proved by our reason . . ."; *DM*, 64: "for . . . the purpose of the philosophers of mechanics . . . it suffices to replace their 'absolute space' by a relative space determined by the heavens of the fixed stars. . . . Motion and rest defined by this relative space can be conveniently used instead of the absolutes. . . .")

(3) The same holds for the word "absolute motion." The principle that all motion is relative can be established by appealing to the meaning of "motion," or else to operationalist arguments. (Cf. *Pr* as above, 58, 115: "To denominate a body 'moved' it is requisite . . . that it changes its distance or situation with regard to some other body . . ."; *DM*, 63: "No motion can be discerned or measured, except with the help of sensible things"; *DM*, 62: ". . . the motion of a stone in a sling or of water in a whirled bucket cannot be called truly circular motion . . . by those who define [motion] with the help of absolute space. . . .")

(4) The words "gravity" and "force" are misused in physics; to introduce force as the cause or "principle" of motion (or of an acceleration) is to introduce "an occult quality" (*DM*, 1–4, and especially 5, 10, 11, 17, 22, 28; *Alc*, vii, 9). More precisely, we should say "an occult metaphysical substance"; for the term "occult quality" is a misnomer, in so far as "quality" should more properly be reserved

for observable or observed qualities—qualities which are given to our
senses, and which, of course, are never "occult." (*An*, 50, Qu. 9; and
especially *DM*, 6: "It is plain, then, that it is useless to assume that the
principle of motion is gravity or force; for how could this principle be
known any more clearly through what has been called an *occult
quality?* That which is itself occult explains nothing. Not to mention
that an unknown acting cause should more properly be called a [meta-
physical] *substance* rather than a *quality*.")

(5) In view of these considerations Newton's theory cannot be
accepted as an explanation which is truly *causal*, i.e. based on true
natural causes. The view that gravity causally explains the motion of
bodies (that of the planets, of free-falling bodies, etc.), or that Newton
discovered that gravity or attraction is "an essential quality" (*Pr*, 106),
whose inherence in the essence or nature of bodies explains the laws of
their motion, must be discarded (*S*, 234; see also *S*, 246, last sentence).
*But it must be admitted that Newton's theory leads to the correct
results* (*DM*, 39, 41). To understand this, "it is of the greatest importance . . . to distinguish between *mathematical hypotheses* and the
natures [*or essences*] *of things*[4] . . . If we observe this distinction,
then all the famous theorems of mechanical philosophy which . . .
make it possible to subject the world system [i.e. the solar system] to
human calculations, may be preserved; and at the same time, the study
of motion will be freed of a thousand pointless trivialities and subtle-
ties, and from [meaningless] abstract ideas" (*DM*, 66).

(6) In physics (mechanical philosophy) there is no causal explanation (cf. *S*, 231), i.e. no explanation based upon the discovery of the
hidden nature or essence of things (*Pr*, 25). ". . . real efficient causes
of the motion . . . of bodies do not in any way belong to the field of
mechanics or of experimental science. Nor can they throw any light
on these . . ." (*DM*, 41).

(7) The reason is, simply, that physical things have no secret or
hidden, "true or real nature," no "real essence," no "internal qualities"
(*Pr*, 101).

(8) There is nothing physical *behind* the physical bodies, no
occult physical reality. *Everything is surface*, as it were; physical
bodies are nothing but their qualities. *Their appearance is their reality*
(*Pr*, 87, 88).

(9) The province of the scientist (of the "mechanical philos-

---

[4] Concerning the equivalence of *"natures"* and *"essences"* see my *Open
Society*, ch. 5, section vi.

opher") is the discovery, "by experiment and reasoning" (*S*, 234), of *Laws of Nature*, that is to say, of the regularities and uniformities of natural phenomena.

(10) The Laws of Nature are, in fact, regularities or similarities or analogies (*Pr*, 105) in the perceived motions of physical bodies (*S*, 234) ". . . these we learn from experience" (*Pr*, 30); they are observed, or inferred from observations (*Pr*, 30, 62; *S*, 228, 264).

(11) "Once the Laws of Nature have been formed, it becomes the task of the philosopher to show of each phenomenon that it is in conformity with these laws, that is, necessarily follows from these principles." (*DM*, 37; cf. *Pr*, 107; and *S*, 231: "their [i.e. the 'mechanical philosophers'] province being . . . to account for particular phenomena by reducing them under, and showing their conformity to, such general rules.")

(12) This process *may* be called, if we like, "explanation" (even "causal explanation"), so long as we distinguish it clearly from the truly causal (i.e. metaphysical) explanation based upon the true nature or essence of things. *S*, 231; *DM*, 37: "A thing may be said to be mechanically explained if it is reduced to those most simple and universal principles" (i.e. "the primary laws of motion which have been proved by experiments . . ." *DM*, 36) "and proved, by accurate reasoning, to be in agreement and connection with them . . . This means to *explain* and solve the phenomena, and to assign them their *cause* . . ." This terminology is admissible (cf. *DM*, 71) but it must not mislead us. We must always clearly distinguish (cf. *DM*, 72) between an "essentialist"[5] explanation with appeals to the nature of things and a "descriptive" explanation which appeals to a Law of Nature, i.e. to the description of an observed regularity. Of these two kinds of explanation only the latter is admissible in physical science.

(13) From both of these we must now distinguish a third kind of "explanation"—an explanation which appeals to *mathematical hypotheses*. A mathematical hypothesis may be described as a procedure for calculating certain results. It is a mere formalism, a mathematical tool or instrument, comparable to a calculating machine. It is judged merely by its efficiency. It may not only be admissible, it may be useful and it may be admirable, yet it is *not science:* even if it produces the correct results, it is only a trick, "a knack" (*An*, 50, Qu. 35). And,

---

[5] The term "essentialist" (and "essentialism") is not Berkeley's but was introduced by me in *The Poverty of Historicism*, and in *The Open Society and Its Enemies*.

as opposed to the explanation by essences (which, in mechanics, are simply false) and to that by laws of nature (which, if the laws "have been proved by experiment," are simply true), the question of the *truth* of a mathematical hypothesis does not arise—only that of its *usefulness as a calculating tool.*

(14) Now, those principles of the Newtonian theory which "have been proved by experiment"—those of the laws of motion which simply describe the observable regularities of the motion of bodies—are true. But the part of the theory involving the concepts which have been criticized above—absolute space, absolute motion, force, attraction, gravity—is not true, since these are "mathematical hypotheses." As such, however, they should not be rejected, if they work well (as in the case of force, attraction, gravity). Absolute space and absolute motion have to be rejected because they do not work (they are to be replaced by the system of fixed stars, and motion relative to it). " 'Force,' 'gravity,' 'attraction,'[6] and words such as these are useful for purposes of reasoning and for computations of motions and of moving bodies; but they do not help us to understand the simple nature of motion itself, nor do they serve to designate so many distinct qualities. . . . As far as attraction is concerned it is clear that it was not introduced by Newton as a true physical quality but merely as a mathematical hypothesis"(*DM*,17).[7]

(15) Properly understood, a mathematical hypothesis does not claim that anything exists in nature which corresponds to it—neither to the words or terms with which it operates, nor to the functional dependencies which it appears to assert. It erects, as it were, a fictitious mathematical world behind that of appearance, but without the claim that this world exists. "But what is said of forces residing in bodies, whether attracting or repelling, is to be regarded only as a mathematical hypothesis, and not as anything really existing in nature" (*S*, 234; cf. *DM*, 18, 39 and especially *Alc*, vii, 9, *An*, 50, Qu. 35). It claims only that from its assumptions the correct consequences can be drawn. But it can easily be misinterpreted as claiming more, as claiming to describe a real world behind the world of appearance. But no such world *could* be described; for the description would necessarily be meaningless.

(16) It can be seen from this that the same appearances *may* be successfully calculated from more than one mathematical hypothesis,

---

[6] The italics in the Latin original function here as quotation marks.

[7] This was more or less Newton's own opinion; cp. Newton's letters to Bentley, 17th January, and especially 25th February 1692-3, and section 3 of ch. 3, above.

and that two mathematical hypotheses which yield the same results concerning the calculated appearances may not only differ, but even contradict each other (especially if they are misinterpreted as describing a world of essences behind the world of appearances); nevertheless, there may be nothing to choose between them. "The foremost of men proffer . . . many different doctrines, and even opposite doctrines, and yet their conclusions [i.e. their calculated results] attain the truth . . . Newton and Torricelli seem to disagree with one another, . . . but the thing is well enough explained by both. For all forces attributed to bodies are merely mathematical hypotheses . . .; thus the same thing may be explained in different ways" (*DM*, 67).

(17) The analysis of Newton's theory thus yields the following results:

We must distinguish

(*a*) Observations of concrete, particular things.

(*b*) Laws of Nature, which are either observations of regularities, or which are proved ("*comprobatae*," *DM*, 36; this may perhaps mean here "supported" or "corroborated"; see *DM*, 31) by experiments, or discovered "by a diligent observation of the phenomena" (*Pr*, 107).

(*c*) Mathematical hypotheses, which are not based on observation but whose consequences agree with the phenomena (or "save the phenomena," as the Platonists said).

(*d*) Essentialist or metaphysical causal explanations, which have no place in physical science.

Of these four, (*a*) and (*b*) are based on observation, and can, from experience, be known to be true; (*c*) is not based on observation and has only an instrumental significance—thus more than one instrument may do the trick (cf. (16), above); and (*d*) is known to be false whenever it constructs a world of essences behind the world of appearances. Consequently (*c*) is also known to be false whenever it is interpreted in the sense of (*d*).

(18) These results clearly apply to cases other than Newtonian theory, for example to atomism (corpuscular theory). In so far as this theory attempts to explain the world of appearances by constructing an invisible world of "inward essences" (*Pr*, 102) behind the world of appearances, it must be rejected. (Cf. *Pr*. 50; *An*, 50; Qu. 56; *S*, 232, 235.)

(19) The work of the scientist leads to something that may be called "explanation," but it is hardly of great value for *understanding* the thing explained, since the attainable explanation is not one based

upon an insight into the nature of things. But it is of practical importance. It enables us to make both *applications* and *predictions*. ". . .
laws of nature or motions direct us how to act, and teach us what to
expect" (*S*, 234; cf. *Pr*, 62). Prediction is based merely upon regular
sequence (not upon causal sequence—at least not in the essentialist
sense). A sudden darkness at noon may be a "prognostic" indicator, a
warning "sign," a "mark" of the coming downpour; nobody takes it as
its cause. Now *all* observed regularities are of this nature even though
"prognostics" or "signs" are usually mistaken for true causes (*TV*,
147; *Pr*, 44, 65, 108; *S*, 252–4; *Alc*, iv, 14, 15).

(20) A general practical result—which I propose to call "Berkeley's razor"—of this analysis of physics allows us *a priori* to eliminate
from physical science all essentialist explanations. If they have a
mathematical and a predictive content they may be admitted *qua*
mathematical hypotheses (while their essentialist interpretation is
eliminated). If not, they may be ruled out altogether. This razor is
sharper than Ockham's: *all* entities are ruled out except those which
are perceived.

(21) The ultimate argument for these views, the reason why
occult substances and qualities, physical forces, structures of cor-
puscles, absolute space, and absolute motion, etc. are eliminated, is
this: we know that there are no entities such as these because we know
that the words professedly designating them must be meaningless. *To
have a meaning, a word must stand for an "idea"*; that is to say, for a
perception, or the memory of a perception; in Hume's terminology,
for an impression or its reflection in our memory. (It may also stand
for a "notion," such as God; but the words belonging to physical
science cannot stand for "notions.") Now the words here in question
do not stand for ideas. "Those who assert that active force, action, and
the principle of motion are in reality inherent in the bodies, maintain a
doctrine that is based upon no experience, and support it by obscure
and general terms, and so do not themselves understand what they
want to say" (*DM*, 31).

Everybody who reads this list of twenty-one theses must be struck by
their modernity. They are surprisingly similar, especially in the criticism of Newton, to the philosophy of physics which Ernst Mach
taught for many years in the conviction that it was new and revolutionary; in which he was followed by, for example, Joseph Petzold;
and which had an immense influence on modern physics, especially on
the Theory of Relativity. There is only one difference: Mach's "prin-

ciple of the economy of thought" (*Denkoekonomie*) goes beyond what I have called "Berkeley's razor," in so far as it allows us not only to discard certain "metaphysical elements," but also to distinguish in some cases between various competing hypotheses (of the kind called by Berkeley "mathematical") with respect to their *simplicity*. (Cf. (16) above.) There is also a striking similarity to Hertz's *Principles of Mechanics* (1894), in which he tried to eliminate the concept of "force," and to Wittgenstein's *Tractatus*.

What is perhaps most striking is that Berkeley and Mach, both great admirers of Newton, criticize the ideas of absolute time, absolute space, and absolute motion, on very similar lines. Mach's criticism, exactly like Berkeley's, culminates in the suggestion that all arguments for Newton's absolute space (like Foucault's pendulum, the rotating bucket of water, the effect of centrifugal forces upon the shape of the earth) fail because these movements are relative to the system of the fixed stars.

To show the significance of this anticipation of Mach's criticism, I may cite two passages, one from Mach and one from Einstein. Mach wrote (in the 7th edition of the *Mechanics*, 1912, ch. ii, section 6, § 11) of the reception of his criticism of *absolute motion*, propounded in earlier editions of his *Mechanics*: "Thirty years ago the view that the notion of 'absolute motion' is meaningless, without any empirical content, and scientifically without use, was generally felt to be very strange. Today this view is upheld by many well-known investigators." And Einstein said in his obituary notice for Mach ("Nachruf auf Mach," *Physikalische Zeitschr.*, 1916), referring to this view of Mach's: "It is not improbable that Mach would have found the Theory of Relativity if, at a time when his mind was still young, the problem of the constancy of velocity of light had agitated the physicists." This remark of Einstein's is no doubt more than generous.[8] Of the bright light it throws upon Mach some reflection must fall upon Berkeley.[9]

A few words may be said about the relation of Berkeley's philosophy of science to his metaphysics. It is very different indeed from Mach's.

---

[8] Mach survived Einstein's Special Theory of Relativity by more than eleven years, at least eight of which were very active years; but he remained strongly opposed to it; and though he alluded to it in the preface to the last (seventh) German edition (1912) of the *Mechanik* published during his lifetime, the allusion was by way of compliment to the opponent of Einstein, Hugo Dingler: Einstein's name and that of the theory were not mentioned.

[9] This is not the place to discuss other predecessors of Mach, such as Leibniz.

While the positivist Mach was an enemy of all traditional, that is nonpositivistic, metaphysics, and especially of all theology, Berkeley was a Christian theologian, and intensely interested in Christian apologetics. While Mach and Berkeley agreed that such words as "absolute time," "absolute space" and "absolute motion" are meaningless and therefore to be eliminated from science, Mach surely would not have agreed with Berkeley on the reason why physics cannot treat of real causes. Berkeley believed in causes, even in "true" or "real" causes; but all true or real causes were to him "efficient or final causes" (*S*, 231), and therefore *spiritual* and utterly beyond physics (cf. *HP*, ii). He also believed in true or real causal *explanation* (*S*, 231) or, as I may perhaps call it, in "ultimate explanation." This, for him, was God.

All appearances are truly caused by God, and explained through God's intervention. This for Berkeley is the simple reason why physics can only describe regularities, and why it cannot find true causes.

It would be a mistake, however, to think that the similarity between Berkeley and Mach is by these differences shown to be only superficial. On the contrary, Berkeley and Mach are both convinced that there is no physical world (of primary qualities, or of atoms; cf. *Pr*, 50; *S*, 232, 235) behind the world of physical appearances (*Pr*, 87, 88). Both believed in a form of the doctrine nowadays called phenomenalism—the view that physical things are bundles, or complexes, or constructs of phenomenal *qualities*, of particular experienced colours, noises, etc.; Mach calls them "complexes of elements." The difference is that for Berkeley, these are directly caused by God. For Mach, they are just there. While Berkley says that there can be nothing physical behind the physical phenomena, Mach suggests that there is nothing at all behind them.

The great historical importance of Berkeley lies, I believe, in his protest against essentialist explanations in science. Newton himself did not interpret his theory in an essentialist sense; he himself did not believe that he had discovered the fact that physical bodies, by their nature, are not only extended but endowed with a force of attraction (radiating from them, and proportional to the amount of matter in them). But soon after him the essentialist interpretation of his theory became the ruling one, and remained so till the days of Mach.

In our own day essentialism has been dethroned; a Berkeleian or Machian positivism or instrumentalism has, after all these years, become fashionable.

Yet there is clearly a third possibility—a "third view" (as I call it).

Essentialism is, I believe, untenable. It implies the idea of an *ultimate* explanation, for an essentialist explanation is neither in need of, nor capable of, further explanation. (If it is in the nature of a body to attract others, then there is no need to ask for an explanation of this fact, and no possibility of finding such an explanation.) Yet we know, at least since Einstein, that explanation may be pushed, unexpectedly, further and further.

But although we must reject essentialism, this does not mean that we have to accept positivism; for we may accept the "third view."

I shall not here discuss the positivist dogma of meaning, since I have done so elsewhere. I shall make only six observations. (i) One can work with something like a world "behind" the world of appearance without committing oneself to essentialism (especially if one assumes that we can never know whether there may not be a further world behind that world). To put it less vaguely, one can work with the idea of hierarchical levels of explanatory hypotheses. There are comparatively low level ones (somewhat like what Berkeley had in mind when he spoke of "Laws of Nature"); higher ones such as Kepler's laws, still higher ones such as Newton's theory, and, next, Relativity. (ii) These theories are not mathematical hypotheses, that is, *nothing but* instruments for the prediction of appearances. Their function goes very much further; for (iii) there is no pure appearance or pure observation: what Berkeley had in mind when he spoke of these things was always the result of interpretation, and (iv) it had therefore a theoretical or hypothetical admixture. (v) New theories, moreover, may lead to re-interpretation of old appearances, and in this way change the world of appearances. (vi) The multiplicity of explanatory theories which Berkeley noted (see Section ii (16), above) is used, wherever possible, to construct, for any two competing theories, conditions in which they yield different observable results, so that we can make a crucial test to decide between them, winning in this way new experience.

A main point of this third view is that science aims at *true* theories, even though we can never be sure that any particular theory is true; and that science *may* progress (and know that it does so) by inventing theories which compared with earlier ones may be described as better approximations to what is true.

So we can now admit, without becoming essentialist, that in

science we always try *to explain the known by the unknown,* the observed (and observable) by the unobserved (and, perhaps, unobservable). At the same time we can now admit, without becoming instrumentalist, what Berkeley said of the nature of hypotheses in the following passage (*S,* 228), which shows both the weakness of his analysis—its failure to realize the conjectural character of all science, including what he calls the "laws of nature"—and also its strength, its admirable understanding of the logical structure of hypothetical explanation.

"It is one thing," Berkeley writes, "to arrive at general laws of nature from a contemplation of the phenomena; and another to frame an hypothesis, and from thence deduce the phenomena. Those who suppose epicycles, and by them explain the motions and appearances of the planets, may not therefore be thought to have discovered principles true in fact and nature. And, albeit we may from the premises infer a conclusion, it will not follow that we can argue reciprocally, and from the conclusion infer the premises. For instance, supposing an elastic fluid, whose constituent minute particles are equidistant from each other, and of equal densities and diameters, and recede one from another with a centrifugal force which is inversely as the distance of the centres; and admitting that from such supposition it must follow that the density and elastic force of such fluid are in the inverse proportion of the space it occupies when compressed by any force; yet we cannot reciprocally infer that a fluid endowed with this property must therefore consist of such supposed equal particles."

BERKELEY'S PHILOSOPHY OF SCIENCE*

T. E. Jessop

. . . Although by academic office primarily engaged in divinity and the biblical and classical languages, Berkeley knew the reformed science from within, both its experimental data and the higher mathematical tools (e.g. the differential calculus) which it had invented for the interpretation of those data. Further, his attitude towards it was sympathetic, not merely critical. He did not come to it as an obscurantist to defend the still lingering Aristotelian tradition, but as a modernist facing modernists, accepting their revolutionary principles and acknowledging the general rightness of their advance. Where he criticised, he did so largely by the standards that had created the new science, i.e. that had given the new science its newness, distinguishing it from both the persisting mediaevalism of most of the universities and the undisciplined revolt against this of the nature-philosophies of the Renaissance. The burden of many of his comments on the modernist physics was that its practitioners should remain more consistently loyal than they had been to its distinctive insights, and that then they would become more acutely aware of its proper intrinsically determined boundaries, knowing exactly what they were doing and not claiming to be proving what their methods could not prove. His reasoned assessment of the new physics was that it was admirable; that it was admirable because, unlike the old physics, its questions and its ways of seeking the answers kept it, when adhered to, from mixing itself with metaphysics; and that when its practitioners strayed from this purity, either by working with obscure concepts of supposedly occult things and powers, or by claiming metaphysical truth for all their conclusions, they spoiled their science, pushing it back towards the old type of physics and thereby tampering with its modernity.

Here, then was an appreciative critique of the new natural science that rested on a comparison of its actual working with its inherent principles, and that set it in a wider context of possible

* From *Hermathena*, XCVII (1963), 23–35. Reprinted by permission of the author and the editors of *Hermathena*.

systematised knowledge. In present-day language, Berkeley had a philosophy of science. The purpose of this paper is to outline this aspect of his thought, to take a glance from this angle only at his brilliant philosophical sallies. . . .

I must now specify a little my characterisation of Berkeley's approach as an examination of the new physics by the latter's own distinctive principles and with a specially sharp eye for its metaphysical assumptions and extrapolations.

On the general scientific attitude that sought the knowledge of Nature through nothing but observation and clear reasoning, without reference or deference to the Greeks, the mediaeval doctors, the Church or anybody else, Berkeley was in entire agreement. Galileo had battled, at heavy cost, for the position that science has no authorities: "What we have to deal with," he wrote caustically, "is the world of our senses, not a world of paper . . . A thousand Aristotles cannot here make true what is false." Berkeley too tilted at those who bowed to "Aristotle hath said it" (*Principles,* Intro., 20). More courageously, he refused to be silenced by "Newton hath said it": "Let Sir Isaac Newton," he wrote to the American Samuel Johnson, "or any other man, be heard only so far as his opinion is supported by reason." And he chides one of his own critics, the Cambridge mathematician Jurin, for trying to settle questions with quotations: "In a matter of mere [pure] science, where authority hath nothing to do, you constantly endeavour to overbear me with authorities."

When *we* look back on the newly born physics we tend to take that attitude for granted, and prefer to define the newness as consisting in a triple conception of method—(1) strenuous insistence on proceeding from observation to theory and checking theory by further observation; (2) observation shall be made where possible under the controlled conditions of experiment; and (3) observation shall take the form of measurement, the reason for this being that the data, being thus quantities, are amenable to the precise, rigorous, self-propagating and therefore almost inexhaustible manipulation of mathematical analysis and synthesis, thereby yielding an intellectually ideal type of theory—pellucidly clear, logically certain, and endlessly resourceful. The wedding of observation and experiment to mathematics through measurement is the summary characterisation of the new thing that sprang up self-consciously and masterfully in Galileo, who announced that we must measure what is measurable and make measurable what is not. This (perhaps *Quanta, semper quanta*) would serve as a better, because technically significant, motto for the Royal Society than the outworn battle-cry which it chose and retains, *Nullius in verba.*

Berkeley's philosophy of science is largely an assessment of this uncompromisingly mathematical type of theory. What he fastens on is its abstractness. It was in order that it *should be* mathematical that observation was sharpened into measurement. The abstractness of physics was thus predetermined at the very first stage of the scientific process, for to measure is to ignore the qualitative aspect of the perceived world. From the start everything we see, touch and hear is reduced to its volume and weight, and all that can happen to volume and weight is at bottom either motion or rest. Theorising necessarily results, then, in a purely mechanistic elucidation of the corporeal universe; everything is to be expressed in terms of space, time, motion, mass and force.

Berkeley did not repudiate this mechanistic physics. He recognised it as a legitimate intellectual adventure, yielding results far clearer, and more cogent and fruitful, than the old qualitative physics. By carving out a homogeneous field of data it made possible an entirely homogeneous theoretical edifice. It was thus, when faithfully worked out, really a science; and so far as it started from measured fact and returned to measured fact, it was a science of corporeal reality, not a piece of merely logical concept-spinning. That, translated into the language natural to our own day, was Berkeley's positive assessment.

His negative assessment, again translated into present day language, was that so selective a science of body could not be the whole or final science of body. To select is to limit, and to limit an inquiry is to limit the truth-value of its conclusions. His negativeness came to the fore because he recognised that this limitation was not being frankly adhered to: some physicists were making claims for a structure reared on observed quantity that were not justified by the limited terms of the system. I shall sketch his treatment of four of these transgressions.

(1) The physicists asserted that corporeal reality consists *only* of volume and weight, and that its behaviour is *only* motion and rest, all other features presented by the senses being subjective, belonging to the perceiving mind, not to the things perceived. This was the point of the distinction between what had recently come to be called the primary and the secondary qualities. The distinction can be found as

far back as Democritus (5th cent. B.C.) but then had a long sleep. It came into modern physics with its founder Galileo, and has remained in it ever since. The philosophers Descartes, Hobbes and Locke endorsed it. The reason Galileo gave for it was that he was quite unable to think of bodily reality without shape, position, motion or rest, but *could* think of it without colour, sound, etc.; and Locke had adduced the same reason. As the conclusion does not seem to me to follow at all from this reason, I think that the operative reason is what Galileo had said earlier in the same work (*Il Saggiatore*), that the "book" of Nature "is written in mathematical language; its signs are triangles, circles and other geometrical figures, without which it is impossible for us to understand a word of it." Whatever we are to make of this pronouncement, the historical fact is that by Berkeley's day the view that the world to which our senses give us access is destitute of colour, sound, taste, smell, heat and cold had become a dogma of both science and philosophy. To believe it was a mark of any educated man's enlightenment. We are expected to believe it still.

So far as I know, Berkeley was the only British scholar of that time at home in both physics and philosophy who framed reasoned objections to that dogma. He indulges in a little banter, in a way that should appeal to our contemporary linguistic philosophers, at the grotesque misuse of language in saying that sound is "really" motion, since this should mean either that sound is never heard, since motion is not, or else that what can be said of sound really applies to motion, in which case we could speak of motion as loud, soft and the like, both these meanings being evidently absurd. This banter apart, he has two repeatedly stressed arguments. (1) It is in fact impossible to imagine anything called body (which is essentially imaginable) without the so-called secondary qualities; e.g. we just cannot have space before the mind without some colour. We can, and physicists do, reason about space without taking any of its colouring into account; but it is one thing to leave colour out of account, a quite different thing to hold that spatial entities have no colour at all. (2) There is no ground for rejecting the plain and stubborn testimony of the senses in respect of colour, sound, etc., and accepting only their testimony in respect of spatial properties and motion. We must accept or reject both together; and if we reject both, the bottom is taken out of any science that insists, as the new physics did, on building on an empirical basis.

Berkeley is not here playing the part of a pretentious meddler with science. He is only holding physics to its proper task when he exposes a dogma that mars its purity. The implicit logical shape of his reasoning is as follows. The doctrine that the corporeal world has *nothing but* spatio-temporal properties is a dogma in the sense that it has no place in the new physics, but is an excrescence upon it. Although laid down by physicists, it is not a proposition that, in its exclusiveness, follows from any other proposition or combination of propositions within physics. A science that restricts itself, as it has a right to do, to the measurable aspects of body has gone beyond its self-limiting brief when it affirms the unreality of the other perceived aspects of body. It should be content to leave what it ignores to some other branch of study. Further, since the dogma raises a question that concerns the truth-status of all empirical sciences whatever, namely, the veracity or inveracity of the senses, it cannot be settled by any one of these sciences singly. It belongs to philosophy, and in his own philosophy Berkeley, refuting scepticism of the senses, believed that he was securing the foundations of empirical science.

(2) Most physicists assumed and some declared that they were discovering the *causes* of corporeal change, and that was what the general public supposed. Also, since the physicists naturally looked for causes only within the corporeal field, and within the measurable part of this, the view was propagated that mechanical causes were the whole and sole causes of all corporeal happenings.

Berkeley threw no doubt on the right of the physicists to keep to their own field and methods. What he did, typically vigilant about logic, was to ask what the physicist really proves when he establishes an alleged causal law, to which his answer, which had been given before and has often been given since, was that when such a law is drawn straight from observation all that has been proved is that so far as the observation has gone one event is uniformly connected with another. That the connection holds good everywhere and always has not been proved (as Hobbes had said, "Experience concludeth nothing universally"), but Berkeley granted that under certain conditions it may fairly be generalised. The result is then a law, but not in the usual sense a causal law, for it has not proved that of the two events so connected one has *produced* the other. It remains a law of mere connection. Physics, then, does not discover causes, for productive power is neither observed in nor rationally deducible from the perceivable properties of bodies, and to posit unperceivable properties is no help, for either these are conceived after the analogy of the perceivable ones, in which case they still provide no basis for production, or else they are mere x's, devoid of content, in which case neither productivity nor anything else can be reasoned out of them.

Berkeley's favourite way of expressing this conclusion was that while there certainly is order in Nature, no *necessity* is discernible in it either by observation or by reason. This is his answer to scientific determinism. There are no corporeal causes. Productive causes must therefore be sought elsewhere. The inquiry, he said, belongs to philosophy, and in his own philosophy he held that causal power is in fact found only in mind: body is merely moved, and only mind can do the moving. The view that body may have what was called "passive power" and mind alone "active power" was in the air at the time (cp. Locke, *Essay*, II, xxiii, 28), and Berkeley contended that the former served all the purposes of physical science.

(3) Physics was much concerned with forces, and it was commonly assumed that forces are obviously causes, and that the laws of their operation are necessary ones.

Berkeley found the physicists' idea of force very confusing. He opens his short treatise *De motu* by mentioning some of the names of its supposed kinds—solicitation (attraction), endeavour, active forces, even dead forces. In *Alciphron* (VII, 6) he compiles a larger list, notes that there had been much disputation over the distinctions and definitions, and remarks that the use of the term "force" is so much a mystery in physics that neither physicists nor the folk that swear by them have any right to scoff at the mysteries in some articles of religion. The term was used for the explanation of changes of motion and the change from motion to rest and *vice versa*. In order to appear in the theoretical structure of the new physics, it had to stand for a quantity. But it was not an observed quantity, yielded by first-hand measurement. It was postulated. How then was its quantity particularised? By being postulated as proportional to the effect to be explained; and as the effect could be directly measured, the postulated force could be calculated from it.

Berkeley put his finger firmly on this device. All that is being done, he said, simplifying in order to lay bare the logic of the procedure, is to take the known quantity of the effect, duplicate it, and call the duplicate the force that has produced the effect. An example he was fond of using was gravity. The observed fact is a falling body. The rest is pure invention. Besides, the mathematical process apart, the invention is not well done, for the notion of force comes from mind, from experience of our own effort, and is unwarrantably transferred to dead stuff: it is a metaphor, and, as Berkeley reminds the readers of his *De motu*, science has no place for metaphors. Further, even if we allow the postulation of an operative force, the specification of it as attraction is arbitrary, since there is nothing observable to indicate whether the force is within the body or outside it, and whether it is a pushing or a pulling one.

Although Berkeley bans the notion of corporeal force from his philosophy, he admits that it has a part to play in a physics dedicated to mathematical terms. From given quantities further ones can be generated and variously manipulated, and some of the results verified within the limits of observation. Theory in the sense both of organisation of data and prediction is thereby promoted, and there are practical applications, as in the devising of machines, which work admirably. But on a rigorous judgement–and science is dishonoured if not judged by rigorous standards–physics has no ground within itself either for taking the quantities invented to be physical realities at all, still less as causes, or for confusing the mathematical necessity of equations with real necessity. Adducing the delightfully neat instance of the parallelogram of forces, he crystallises his criticism in the simple remark, "to be of service to reckoning and mathematical demonstrations is one thing, to set forth the nature of things is another" (*De motu*, 18, Luce's trans.). The first is a domestic affair of physics, the second a leap outside that exposes it to philosophical criticism.

That is what Berkeley meant by calling forces "mathematical hypotheses" (*De motu*, 67). In his own philosophy he gives reasons for holding that in a theory of reality more widely based than physics they are unrequired. In *Siris* (290; cp. 249f.) he calls them "phantoms," and puts them in the same class as "absolute motions and real spaces," which "do pass in physics for causes and principles, yet are they in truth but hypotheses, nor can they be objects of real science" [i.e. the science of what is real].

(4) The physicists' doctrine of space and time troubled Berkeley. I can merely touch on the subject very generally. In the older physics the centre of interest was in corporeal things and their own properties, space and time being considered as little more than attendant circumstances. In the new physics they became important factors; for instance, the fall of bodies was expressed as a function not

of weight but of the time of the fall. Further, as the new physics had unified celestial and terrestrial dynamics, the relativity of motions observed from an earth that both spins on its axis and moves in a large orbit round the sun became a pressing problem. The idea of an absolute motion involves the ideas of an absolute space and an absolute time, and Newton had adopted them, in his case to define the sense in which the principle of motion in a straight line—an article of his first law of motion—could be read unambiguously. There was also the old problem of whether space and time are finite or infinite, and whether they are finitely or infinitely divisible, this latter problem being raised afresh by the use of infinitesimals in Newton's method of fluxions.

It may rightly be said that Berkeley put himself on the side of finitude of both extent and divisibility, but the deeper point is that he dismissed the problems as false ones, for his main contention was that when space and time are cut away from bodies and events and are reduced to a pure and empty framework they are fictions, so that the question whether or no they are really infinite and infinitely divisible does not arise. Berkeley is here again drawing attention to the obscurities, created difficulties, and metaphysically questionable steps to which a physics at once bound and loosened (i.e. tethered and yet given a wonderfully long rope) by a mathematical technique is always liable, and which therefore it should be vigilant to avoid. It is worth observing that, after Berkeley, Kant, who had been a physicist before he became a philosopher, came to a somewhat similar conclusion.

In this account, not of Berkeley's general philosophy and of all his motives, but of his direct confrontation with the current physics, the picture emerges of a man who knew the science he was examining and wanted it to progress, but faced it with a philosopher's awareness that every special science is limited by its very specialism, that its basic concepts, methods and criteria restrict both the kinds of fact it can handle and the sense in which, or the degree to which, it can claim real truth for the ascending stages, of its theoretical superstructure. In the case of physics he maintained that the wedding of a science of fact with mathematics was not, if real truth be the test, a wholly happy one, for mathematics, being an abstract system developed independently of sensible facts, is always prone in that alliance both to mistake some of its symbols for really existing or operative entities, and to impose on given facts its own inner and purely logical necessities.

How far Berkeley's philosophy of science needs to be modified by the *new* new physics which, in its wizardry of theory and its spectacular applications, is astonishing us now, I am not competent to say. I can only note that while this newest physics is far more subtly mathematical than Newton's, its leaders are much less inclined to claim real or ultimate truth-value for its ethereally abstract theories than the disciples of Newton were for theirs, and that the new system, unlike the earlier one, has not suggested to the speculatively minded anything like a materialistic determinism. Besides, it is a far less stable system than Newton's, which lasted with little change for about two hundred years: already it is in full flight, romping from one exciting change to another and riven with deep controversies. I would add this reason to my Berkeleian misgivings about mathematical abstraction and mathematical necessity to excuse my own reluctance to attempt to build on current physics a metaphysic of the corporeal universe.

PRIMARY AND SECONDARY QUALITIES

OF THE OBJECTS OF PERCEPTION;
AND, FIRST, OF PRIMARY
AND SECONDARY QUALITIES*

Thomas Reid (1710–1792)

The objects of perception are the various qualities of bodies. Intending to treat of these only in general, and chiefly with a view to explain the notions which our senses give us of them, I begin with the distinction between primary and secondary qualities. These were distinguished very early. The Peripatetic system confounded them, and left no difference. The distinction was again revived by Des Cartes and Locke, and a second time abolished by Berkeley and Hume. If the real foundation of this distinction can be pointed out, it will enable us to account for the various revolutions in the sentiments of philosophers concerning it.

Every one knows that extension, divisibility, figure, motion, solidity, hardness, softness, and fluidity, were by Mr. Locke called *primary qualities of body;* and that sound, colour, taste, smell, and heat or cold, were called *secondary qualities.* Is there a just foundation for this distinction? Is there anything common to the primary which belongs not to the secondary? And what is it?

I answer, that there appears to me to be a real foundation for the distinction; and it is this—that our senses give us a direct and a distinct notion of the primary qualities, and inform us what they are in themselves. But of the secondary qualities, our senses give us only a relative and obscure notion. They inform us only, that they are qualities that affect us in a certain manner—that is, produce in us a certain sensation; but as to what they are in themselves, our senses leave us in the dark.

Every man capable of reflection may easily satisfy himself that he has a perfectly clear and distinct notion of extension, divisibility, figure, and motion. The solidity of a body means no more but that it excludes other bodies from occupying the same place at the same time. Hardness, softness, and fluidity are different degrees of cohesion in the parts of a body. It is fluid when it has no sensible cohesion; soft, when

---

* From Reid's *Essay on the Intellectual Powers of Man,* 1785, chap. XVII.

112

the cohesion is weak; and hard, when it is strong. Of the cause of this cohesion we are ignorant, but the thing itself we understand perfectly, being immediately informed of it by the sense of touch. It is evident, therefore, that of the primary qualities we have a clear and distinct notion; we know what they are, though we may be ignorant of their causes.

I observed, farther, that the notion we have of primary qualities is direct, and not relative only. A relative notion of a thing, is strictly speaking, no notion of the thing at all, but only of some relation which it bears to something else.

Thus, gravity sometimes signifies the tendency of bodies towards the earth; sometimes it signifies the cause of that tendency. When it means the first, I have a direct and distinct notion of gravity; I see it, and feel it, and know perfectly what it is; but this tendency must have a cause. We give the same name to the cause; and that cause has been an object of thought and of speculation. Now, what notion have we of this cause when we think and reason about it? It is evident we think of it as an unknown cause, of a known effect. This is a relative notion; and it must be obscure, because it gives us no conception of what the thing is, but of what relation it bears to something else. Every relation which a thing unknown bears to something that is known, may give a relative notion of it; and there are many objects of thought and of discourse of which our faculties can give no better than a relative notion.

Having premised these things to explain what is meant by a relative notion, it is evident that our notion of primary qualities is not of this kind; we know what they are, and not barely what relation they bear to something else.

It is otherwise with secondary qualities. If you ask me, what is that quality or modification in a rose which I call its smell, I am at a loss to answer directly. Upon reflection, I find, that I have a distinct notion of the sensation which it produces in my mind. But there can be nothing like to this sensation in the rose, because it is insentient. The quality in the rose is something which occasions the sensation in me; but what that something is, I know not. My senses give me no information upon this point. The only notion, therefore, my senses give is this—that smell in the rose is an unknown quality or modification, which is the cause or occasion of a sensation which I know well. The relation which this unknown quality bears to the sensation with which nature hath connected it, is all I learn from the sense of smelling; but this is evidently a relative notion. The same reasoning will apply to every secondary quality.

Thus, I think it appears that there is a real foundation for the distinction of primary from second qualities; and that they are distinguished by this—that of the primary we have by our senses a direct and distinct notion; but of the secondary only a relative notion, which must, because it is only relative, be obscure; they are conceived only as the unknown causes or occasions of certain sensations with which we are well acquainted.

The account I have given of this distinction is founded upon no hypothesis. Whether our notions of primary qualities are direct and distinct, those of the secondary relative and obscure, is a matter of fact, of which every man may have certain knowledge by attentive reflection upon them. To this reflection I appeal, as the proper test of what has been advanced, and proceed to make some reflections on this subject.

1. The primary qualities are neither sensations, nor are they resemblances of sensations. This appears to me self-evident. I have a clear and distinct notion of each of the primary qualities. I have a clear and distinct notion of sensation. I can compare the one with the other; and, when I do so, I am not able to discern a resembling feature. Sensation is the act or the feeling (I dispute not which) of a sentient being. Figure, divisibility, solidity, are neither acts nor feelings. Sensation supposes a sentient being as its subject; for a sensation that is not felt by some sentient being, is an absurdity. Figure and divisibility supposes a subject that is figured and divisible, but not a subject that is sentient.

2. We have no reason to think that any of the secondary qualities resemble any sensation. The absurdity of this notion has been clearly shown by Des Cartes, Locke, and many modern philosophers. It was a tenet of the ancient philosophy, and is still by many imputed to the vulgar, but only as a vulgar error. It is too evident to need proof, that the vibrations of a sounding body do not resemble the sensation of sound, nor the effluvia of an odorous body the sensation of smell.

3. The distinctness of our notions of primary qualities prevents all questions and disputes about their nature. There are no different opinions about the nature of extension, figure, or motion, or the nature

of any primary quality. Their nature is manifest to our senses, and cannot be unknown to any man, or mistaken by him, though their causes may admit of dispute.

The primary qualities are the object of the mathematical sciences; and the distinctness of our notions of them enables us to reason demonstratively about them to a great extent. Their various modifications are precisely defined in the imagination, and thereby capable of being compared, and their relations determined with precision and certainty.

It is not so with secondary qualities. Their nature not being manifest to the sense, may be a subject of dispute. Our feeling informs us that the fire is hot; but it does not inform us what that heat of the fire is. But does it not appear a contradiction, to say we know that the fire is hot, but we know not what that heat is? I answer, there is the same appearance of contradiction in many things that must be granted. We know that wine has an inebriating quality; but we know not what that quality is. It is true, indeed, that, if we had not some notion of what is meant by the heat of fire, and by an inebriating quality, we could affirm nothing of either with understanding. We have a notion of both; but it is only a relative notion. We know that they are the causes of certain known effects.

4. The nature of secondary qualities is a proper subject of philosophical disquisition; and in this philosophy has made progress. It has been discovered, that the sensation of smell is occasioned by the effluvia of bodies; that of sound by their vibration. The disposition of bodies to reflect a particular kind of light, occasions the sensation of colour. Very curious discoveries have been made of the nature of heat, and an ample field of discovery in these subjects remains.

5. We may see why the sensations belonging to secondary qualities are an object of our attention, while those which belong to the primary are not.

The first are not only signs of the object perceived, but they bear a capital part in the notion we form of it. We conceive it only as that which occasions such a sensation, and therefore cannot reflect upon it without thinking of the sensation which it occasions; we have no other mark whereby to distinguish it. The thought of a secondary quality, therefore, always carries us back to the sensation which it produces. We give the same name to both, and are apt to confound them together.

But having a clear and distinct conception of primary qualities, we have no need, when we think of them, to recall their sensations. When a primary quality is perceived, the sensation immediately leads our thought to the quality signified by it, and is itself forgot. We have no occasion afterwards to reflect upon it; and so we come to be as little acquainted with it as if we had never felt it. This is the case with the sensations of all primary qualities, when they are not so painful or pleasant as to draw our attention.

When a man moves his hand rudely against a pointed hard body, he feels pain, and may easily be persuaded that this pain is a sensation, and that there is nothing resembling it in the hard body; at the same time he perceives the body to be hard and pointed, and he knows that these qualities belong to the body only. In this case, it is easy to distinguish what he feels from what he perceives.

Let him again touch the pointed body gently, so as to give him no pain; and now you can hardly persuade him that he feels anything but the figure and hardness of the body; so difficult it is to attend to the sensations belonging to primary qualities, when they are neither pleasant nor painful. They carry the thought to the external object, and immediately disappear and are forgot. Nature intended them only as signs; and when they have served that purpose they vanish.

We are now to consider the opinions both of the vulgar and of philosophers upon this subject. As to the former, it is not to be expected that they should make distinctions which have no connection with the common affairs of life; they do not, therefore, distinguish the primary from the secondary qualities, but speak of both as being equally qualities of the external object. Of the primary qualities they have a distinct notion, as they are immediately and distinctly, perceived by the senses; of the secondary, their notions, as I apprehend, are confused and indistinct, rather than erroneous. A secondary quality is the unknown cause or occasion of a well-known effect; and the same name is common to the cause and the effect. Now, to distinguish clearly the different ingredients of a complex notion, and, at the same time, the different meanings of an ambiguous word, is the work of a philosopher; and is not to be expected of the vulgar, when their occasions do not require it.

I grant, therefore, that the notion which the vulgar have of secondary qualities, is indistinct and inaccurate. But there seems to be a contradiction between the vulgar and the philosopher upon this subject, and each charges the other with a gross absurdity. The vulgar say, that fire is hot, and snow cold, and sugar sweet; and that to deny this is a gross absurdity, and contradicts the testimony of our senses. The philosopher says that heat, and cold, and sweetness, are nothing but sensations in our minds; and it is absurd to conceive that these sensations are in the fire, or in the snow, or in the sugar.

I believe this contradiction, between the vulgar and the philosopher, is more apparent than real; and that it is owing to an abuse of language on the part of the philosopher, and to indistinct notions on the part of the vulgar. The philosopher says, there is no heat in the fire, meaning that the fire has not the sensation of heat. His meaning is just, and the vulgar will agree with him, as soon as they understand his meaning: but his language is improper; for there is really a quality in the fire, of which the proper name is heat, and the name of heat is given to this quality, both by philosophers and by the vulgar, much more frequently than to the sensation of heat. This speech of the philosopher, therefore, is meant by him in one sense; it is taken by the vulgar in another sense. In the sense in which they take it, it is indeed absurd, and so they hold it to be. In the sense in which he means it, it is true; and the vulgar, as soon as they are made to understand that sense, will acknowledge it to be true. They know, as well as the philosopher, that the fire does not feel heat; and this is all that he means by saying there is no heat in the fire.

The external senses have a double province—to make us feel, and to make us perceive. They furnish us with a variety of sensations, some pleasant, others painful, and others indifferent; at the same time, they give us a conception and an invincible belief of the existence of external objects. This conception of external objects is the work of nature; so likewise is the sensation that accompanies it. This conception and belief which nature produces by means of the senses, we call *perception*. The feeling which goes along with the perception, we call *sensation*. The perception and its corresponding sensation are produced at the same time. In our experience we never find them disjoined. Hence, we are led to consider them as one thing, to give them one name, and to confound their different attributes. It becomes very difficult to separate them in thought, to attend to each by itself, and to attribute nothing to it which belongs to the other.

To do this, requires a degree of attention to what passes in our own minds, and a talent of distinguishing things that differ, which is not to be expected in the vulgar, and is even rarely found in philosophers; so that the progress made in a just analysis of the operations of our senses has been very slow. The hypothesis of ideas, so generally adopted, hath, as I apprehend, greatly retarded this progress, and we might hope for a quicker advance, if philosophers could so far humble themselves as to believe that, in every branch of the philosophy of nature, the productions of human fancy and conjecture will be found to be dross; and that the only pure metal that will endure the test, is what is discovered by patient observation and chaste induction.

SUBSTANCE, REALITY,
AND PRIMARY QUALITIES*

Jonathan Bennett

Two bad mistakes have been taken over from Berkeley by most philosophers who have read and assessed him with the casualness usually accorded to the great, dead philosophers. Each mistake is in the nature of a conflation or running together of two philosophical doctrines which ought to be kept apart, and thus a conflation also of the problems which the doctrines offer to solve. The doctrines in question are all expounded in Locke's *Essay Concerning Human Understanding*. They are: (1) a certain account of what it is for a property to be instantiated by something; (2) a certain account of the distinction between appearance and reality, or between how it is with me and how it is with the world; and (3) a thesis about primary and secondary qualities. Locke certainly accepted (2) and (3). His scathing attacks on (1) have usually been taken as a defence of it—here Locke has suffered the usual fate of the ironist.

In Part I, I shall discuss the conflation by Berkeley and others of (1) with (2). This conflation is, specifically, an *identification*: Berkeley actually failed to see that (1) and (2) are distinct. The conflation of (2) with (3)—which I shall treat in Part II—has not usually taken the extreme form of an identifying of the two doctrines with one another. Occasionally, (3) is described as a "version" of (2), but a more common mistake is the milder one of treating (3) as being integrally connected with (2) in a way in which it is not.

PART I

1. *The Substance Doctrine.* The account of property-instantiation which I call "Lockean," meaning that Locke said a good deal about it, is a view about the logic of subject-predicate statements. What concepts—or, as Locke would put it, what *ideas*—are involved

* From *American Philosophical Quarterly*, II, No. 1 (1965), 1–17. Reprinted by permission of the author and the editor of *American Philosophical Quarterly*.

in the subject of the statement that *The pen in my hand is expensive*? Certainly, the concepts of being a pen, and of being in my hand; but these are not enough, for the statement speaks of a *thing which* is a pen and is in my hand. What thing is this? I may answer that it is the purple thing which I now see before me; but when I say that the purple thing I now see is a pen and is in my hand, I speak of a *thing which* is purple, etc., and so my introduction of "purple" and "seen by me" still fails to capture the whole concept of the subject in the original statement. Even if I produce some nontrivial truth of the form "The . . . is purple, is seen by me, and is a pen in my hand," this can be only a delaying action. Sooner or later, I must admit that this kind of expansion is bound to omit an essential element from the concept of the pen in my hand. What is missing is the concept of a *thing which* . . .: this is an ingredient in the concept of a *thing which is F* for each value of *F*, and is therefore not identical with the concept of a *thing which is F* for any value of *F*. This omnipresent constituent of any subject-concept is the concept of a property-bearer, or of a possible subject of predication. Let us call it the concept of a *substance*. It appears then that if any subject-predicate—or any existential—statements are true, there must be two basic sorts of item: (a) substances, and (b) qualities or properties. It is the special privilege of substances that they can bear or have or support qualities, and cannot in the same way be borne by anything else. We commit ourselves to the existence of "substances" in this sense every time we affirm of some property that it is instantiated by something or other: for a property to be instantiated is for there to be some substance which has or bears it.

I offer the foregoing paragraph as a rational reconstruction of one strand in the substantialism which Locke discusses in *Essay* II, xxiii, 1–4. In sec. 2 he says: "The idea then we have, to which we give the general name substance, being nothing but the supposed but unknown support of those qualities we find existing, which, we imagine, cannot subsist *sine re substante*, without something to support them, we call that support *substantia*, which, according to the true import of the word is, in plain English, standing under, or upholding." It is usual for Locke to say that we cannot "imagine" how qualities or accidents can exist unsupported, but the substantialism in question is certainly based, at least in part, upon logical considerations: some awareness of this is shown by Locke in II, xii, 4 and III, vi, 21, though the latter is not quite consistent.

Leibniz made a good remark about the Lockean theory of

property-instantiation: "In distinguishing two things in [any] substance, the attributes or predicates, and the common subject of these
predicates, it is no wonder that we can conceive nothing particular in
this subject. It must be so, indeed, since we have already separated
from it all the attributes in which we could conceive any detail" (*New
Essays* II, xxiii, 2). This suggests, though it did not to Leibniz, the
following argument. Suppose a substantialist were to say that any
given item counts as a substance if and only if it has a certain property
S which is definitive of substantiality. In that case, his account of what
it is for a property to be instantiated, viz., that P is instantiated if and
only if some substance bears P, would say merely that P is instantiated
if and only if some item is both S and P. His analysis of a statement
about the instantiation of one property would thus yield, uselessly, a
statement about the joint instantiation of two properties. A defender
of the Lockean doctrine must therefore deny that substances are items
of a certain kind; to be of a kind is to have the properties which define
the kind, and the Lockean doctrine cannot allow that there are properties which substances must have in order to count as substances. But
the claim that substances are items of a certain kind *is* the Lockean
account of property-instantiation. The whole point and interest of the
account lies in its claim that every subject-concept includes the
concept of a certain kind of item whose special right and duty it is to
bear properties.

The Lockean account must, therefore, be wrong. There is,
perhaps, a "concept of a subject in general," but it is to be elucidated
in terms of the way in which more special concepts function in certain
kinds of statement, and is not to be regarded as a concept which picks
out a class of items.

2. *The Veil-of-Perception Doctrine.* Locke certainly did make a
mistake about the distinction between what appears to be the case and
what is really, or objectively, the case. His view is that the difference
between seeing a tree, say, and being in a visual state as of seeing a tree
though there is no tree to be seen, is the difference between having a
sensory "idea" while in the presence of a real thing which is like the
idea, and having such an idea while in the presence of no such thing.
Sometimes he speaks only of a "correspondence," "agreement," or
"conformity" between the sensory idea and the thing; and he also
thinks that there is a causal relation between the two; but he speaks too
of a "likeness," and of ideas as "copies" of real things. This exposed
him to a damaging attack from Berkeley who said that "An idea can be

like nothing but an idea," and that no sense attaches to the question whether human sensory states are informative of a real, objective world which is *like* them. This talk about ideas as like real things is associated with, and strongly reinforces, Locke's mistaken handling of the question "Might it not be the case that there are no real things at all outside my mind? Can I be sure that the whole course of my experience is not just a dream?" Locke tries repeatedly to lay these sceptical doubts: see IV, ii, 14; iv, 4–5; and xi, 2–10. His arguments to this end are unsatisfactory, consisting as they do of *ad hominem* teasing of the sceptic and covert appeals to empirical evidence. Even opponents of phenomenalism would now hesitate, I think, to follow Locke in his calm assumption that the question "Might it not be that there is no real extra-mental world?" requires an answer but stands in no need of criticism. Locke criticizes the moral character of the questioner, but his picture of the real world as represented by sensory states which "copy" it precludes his criticizing the question. This aspect of Locke's thought may be summed up in the remark that Locke puts the real world on the other side of the veil of perception, which explains my phrase "veil-of-perception doctrine." The word "doctrine" is misleading, though. Locke's treatment of the appearance/reality distinction is not prominent in the *Essay*: it appears mainly as a by-product of the mishandling of a certain sceptical question, and it has little of the weight or the deliberateness which go with a properly doctrinal status.

3. *The Two Doctrines in Berkeley*. The two philosophical views which I have sketched are distinct: one addresses itself to the question "What concepts do we use when we say *Something is F?*" while the other tackles the question "What is the difference between saying that *It is as though I were seeing a tree* and saying that *I see a tree?*" Although these are as different as chalk from cheese, Berkeley confidently identified them.

In *Principles* sec. 49 he discusses the logical doctrine of substance without bringing in the veil-of-perception doctrine; and in sec. 18–20, 86–88 there is a good part of the case against the latter, with no admixture of polemic against substance. But nearly always Berkeley welds the two doctrines together to form a single view about "material substance." Berkeley uses "matter" and its cognates to refer to Locke's purported "real things" which lie behind the veil of perception. (He also associates "matter" with Locke's views about primary qualities, but that raises issues which I shall discuss in Part II.) The word "substance," on the other hand, is especially associated with the Lockean account of property-instantiation. The phrase "material substance," then, which Berkeley uses lavishly and which hardly occurs in Locke, ensures that any discussion of one of the two doctrines has a good chance of becoming mixed up with a discussion of the other. Sometimes the mixture is fairly innocent, as in *Principles* sec. 68, for example; but often it is lethal. In *Principles* sec. 16 Berkeley makes a point about substance, and not only refers to it as "matter" but also invokes "extension," which has nothing in particular to do with substratum-substance but does have to do with primary qualities and also with Locke's real world beyond the veil of perception: "It is said extension is a mode or accident of matter, and that matter is the substratum that supports it. Now I desire you that you would explain what is meant by matter's *supporting* extension. . . ."

Again, in sec. 17 Berkeley tries to locate the enemy: "If we inquire into what the most accurate philosophers declare themselves to mean by *material substance*, we shall find they acknowledge they have no other meaning annexed to those sounds but the idea of being in general, together with the relative notion of its supporting accidents." This is a fair enough report of what Locke says not about "material substance" but about "substance." Berkeley adds that he does not understand the proffered account of the "meaning annexed to these sounds," and continues: "But why should we trouble ourselves any further in discussing this material *substratum* or support of figure and motion and other sensible qualities? Does it not suppose they have an existence without the mind? And is not this a direct repugnancy and altogether inconceivable?" He then launches off from "existence without the mind," etc., into an attack on the veil-of-perception doctrine! In this passage, a complaint against a wrong analysis of subject-concepts is jumbled together with a complaint against Locke's insufficiently idealist analysis of reality.

In sec. 37: "If the word *substance* be taken in the vulgar sense, for a combination of sensible qualities, such as extension, solidity, weight and the like: this we cannot be accused of taking away. But if it be taken in a philosophic sense, for the support of accidents or qualities without the mind; then indeed I acknowledge that we take it away, if one may be said to take away that which never had any existence, not even in the imagination." This might be taken to mean "Of course there are things which have properties, but in saying this we do not employ a concept of naked thinghood"; or it might be taken to mean "Of course there are real objects, but that statement can be analyzed purely in terms of mental states." There is no basis for preferring either interpretation. (See also sec. 74, 76.)

These are some of the clearer expressions of the conflation; but the *Principles* and *Three Dialogues* contain many others which would suit my purpose even better if they did not also involve the further tangling of the two views so far discussed with Locke's view about primary qualities.

4. *Why Berkeley Identified the Two Doctrines*. This is not just a simple-minded blunder on Berkeley's part. His identification of the two Lockean doctrines flows naturally from his underlying assumption that the word "idea" can be used univocally to cover something in the nature of sensory states and something in the nature of concepts or meanings of words. This assumption enables Berkeley to use "ideas of things" in such a way as to identify *qualities of things* with *sensory states which we have when we perceive things*. An idea of white for example is a certain kind of visual field; but it is also what I must be able to have in my mind if I am to understand the word "white," i.e., it is the meaning of the word "white," i.e., it is the property or quality of whiteness.

Since Berkeley uses "idea" in these two ways, it is natural that he should fail to distinguish the two Lockean doctrines; for each doctrine purports to offer an anchor for free-floating "ideas," one relating sensory states to the objectively real, and the other relating qualities to the things which have them. Furthermore, Berkeley can say of each Lockean doctrine that it over-populates the world: one by postulating "real things" which are logically dissociated from ideas (=sensory states), and the other by postulating "substances" which are something over and above collections of ideas (=qualities).

This diagnosis of the conflation is strongly confirmed in *Principles* sec. 78: "Qualities . . . are nothing else but *sensations* or *ideas*, which exist only in a mind perceiving them." (See also *Principles* sec. 9.)

Special note should be taken of the phrase "sensible qualities," in which Berkeley often embodies his double use of "idea." For example in sec. 38: "But, say you, it sounds very harsh to say we eat and drink ideas, and are clothed with ideas. I acknowledge it does so, the word *idea* not being used in common discourse to signify the several combinations of sensible qualities which are called *things*. . . . But . . . the hardness or softness, the colour, taste, warmth and such like qualities which combined together constitute the several sorts of victuals and apparel, have been shown to exist only in the mind that perceives them; and this is all that is meant by calling them *ideas*. . . ."

5. *The Two Doctrines in Locke.* The source of Berkeley's identification of the two doctrines is his double use of "idea"; but this he shares with Locke. Yet Locke does not run the substance doctrine together with the veil-of-perception doctrine: the two are distinct in Locke, as well as in fact. Since their nondistinctness does more or less follow from a premiss which Locke accepts—namely that "idea of *x*" can without ambiguity mean both "quality of *x*" and "appearance of *x*"–it must be conceded that Locke keeps the two doctrines apart only by betraying his basic premisses. This picture of Locke, as saying something true which he is committed to denying, is confirmed by certain details in the relevant parts of the *Essay*. These parts are not extensive; but they do show that, although Locke has no intention of identifying the substance doctrine with the veil-of-perception doctrine, he cannot help expounding the former in words which would also be appropriate to the latter. In his handling of the two doctrines, they drift together of their own accord.

(1) In the opening sections of *Essay* II, xxiii, Locke speaks of substance as something which we invoke when we become aware of "a certain number of simple ideas which go constantly together," or as something which is supposed to uphold "such combinations of simple ideas as are by experience and the observation of men's senses taken notice of to exist together." These expressions have to do with the instantiation of properties only if "idea" is taken to mean something like "property." But then, it seems, Locke is here raising not the general question "What is it for a property to be instantiated?" but the much more special question "What is it for a number of properties which go constantly together to be jointly instantiated?" This shift is bewildering; but it becomes intelligible if we remember that "ideas" may also be sensory states. For if we take "idea" to mean "sensory state," the phrases "ideas which go constantly together" and "combinations of simple ideas [which] exist together" may be taken to refer to certain kinds of dependable order in our experience. On that interpretation, the passages in question do not concern a queerly restricted version of the substratum-substance doctrine but rather concern the problems about objectivity or "reality" which are the province of the veil-of-perception doctrine. Locke makes no attempt overtly to connect substance with what lies behind the veil-of-perception; but the basis for such a connection is there in the words he uses.

(2) In II, xxiii, 1, Locke says that when we note a number of

sensory ideas going together, "not imagining how these simple ideas can subsist by themselves, we accustom ourselves to suppose some substratum wherein they do subsist and from which they do result; which, therefore, we call substance." Here again, substances are supposed to uphold "ideas"; and ideas must again be properties if the passage is to concern the substance doctrine at all. But, so construed, the passage says that substances are supposed to *cause* their own properties, and it is not clear why Locke should have thought that anyone believes that. Our puzzlement is removed if we remember that ideas can also be sensory states; for, on that reading of "from which [ideas] do result," it echoes that part of the veil-of-perception doctrine which says that real things cause our sensory states. As in the previous case, Locke here declines to exploit this verbal overlap between the two doctrines in order explicitly to identify them with one another. On the contrary, in the very next section he tries to drag "ideas" apart from "qualities," and thus to free the substance doctrine of any talk about causal relations by asserting that substances support qualities and that qualities cause sensory states: "If anyone will examine himself concerning his notion of pure substance in general, he will find he has no other idea of it at all, but only a supposition of he knows not what support of such qualities which are capable of producing simple ideas in us."

(3) In II, xii, 4–6, Locke first distinguishes between "ideas of modes" and "ideas of substances." He clearly intends this to correspond to a distinction between adjectives and nouns, or between what may be said of a thing and things of which something may be said. This purely logical interpretation of the mode/substance distinction reappears at intervals throughout the *Essay*, for example in II, xiii, 19: "They who first ran into the notion of accidents, as a sort of real beings that needed something to inhere in, were forced to find out the word substance to support them," a remark which contains no hint of a restriction to substances of the special kind which Locke calls "real things." Yet even in his first introduction of "ideas of substances" and of the allegedly associated "supposed, or confused, idea of substance, such as it is," there is a dangerous reference to "distinct particular things subsisting by themselves." This last phrase could be taken to mean "things which exist independently of any percipient," an interpretation which would connect "ideas of substances" with the veil-of-perception doctrine. Perhaps in that passage Locke is not taking "subsisting by themselves" in that way; but he certainly does so later. In II,

xxx, 4, he says, in effect, that in constructing complex ideas of modes we are subject only to the laws of logic: "There is nothing more required to those kinds of ideas to make them real, but that they be so framed, that there be a possibility of existing conformable to them." In the next section, however, he says that ideas of substances are subject to a more stringent requirement: "Our complex ideas of substances being made, all of them, in reference to things existing without us, and intended to be representations of substances as they really are, are no farther real than as they are such combinations of simple ideas as are really united and co-exist in things without us." This is a mistake: the propriety of a general noun no more depends upon its having instances than does the propriety of an adjective. My point, however, is that in making this mistake Locke very explicitly connects "ideas of substances" with questions about appearance and reality, and thus lays the foundation for connecting the latter with the doctrine of substratum-substance. I say only that he "lays the foundation" for this, because in this passage which so explicitly connects ideas of *substances* with "things without us" there is, interestingly, no mention at all of the idea of *substance*.

On this evidence, I think we may say that Locke did not wish to identify the two doctrines but was under pressure from his own presuppositions to do so.

6. *Why Others Have Identified the Two Doctrines.* So much for Berkeley and Locke; but what of those philosophers who have collapsed the substance doctrine into the veil-of-perception doctrine without having the excuse of an underlying mistake about the use of "idea"? The following hypothesis may help to explain their mistake.

One considers the distinction between appearance and reality and illustrates it by: "It seems to me that I see something square, but is there really something square which I see?" One then puts this in the form: "I am in the presence of a manifestation, in my visual field, of squareness; but am I in the presence of something which is square?" The question whether what appears to be the case is really the case is thus quietly transmuted into the question whether a certain property has a possessor. One notes also that each question might—mistakenly but plausibly—be analyzed in terms of an elusive "something we know not what," and this further encourages one to believe that they are two versions of a single question of which Locke gave a single wrong analysis.

The train of thought indicated in my hypothesis is invalid. The question "Given that I seem to see something square, is there really something square which I see?" does not raise the question about property-instantiation which the Lockean doctrine of substance is supposed to elucidate. This is proved by a simple destructive dilemma.

(a) If we allow that my visual field contains a part which is square, then that part is the "thing which" is square, i.e., it bears the property of squareness with which I am confronted. It is a mistake to think that the Lockean concept of substance must be so handled that only physical or public or extra-mental objects are cases of substance-plus-properties. The whole point of the doctrine, as is often remarked, is that it separates the substance from *all* its properties and insists that for a property to be instantiated is for it to be borne by an item of which nothing can be said except that it bears that property. So: *if some part of my visual field is square, then I am not in the presence of a property for which I am seeking a bearer*, for the property in whose presence I am already has a bearer.

(b) If, more sensibly, we deny that anything in my visual field is itself square, and say only that my visual field is similar to ones which I often have when I see something square, then my agnosticism about whether I see a square thing is agnosticism about whether I am in the presence of a manifestation of squareness at all. My question "Is the world at this point really as it appears to be?" is therefore not of the form "Is there a bearer for this property?" So: *if no part of my visual field is square, then I am not in the presence of a property for which I am seeking a bearer*, for I am not, in the required sense, "in the presence of a property" at all.

7. *Some Examples.* Here is one passage where Berkeley makes the shift I have described from "Does something real correspond to this sensory state?" to "Does something have this property?"

It is worth while to reflect a little on the motives which induced men to suppose the existence of material substance. . . . First, therefore, it was thought that colour, figure, motion, and the rest of the sensible qualities or accidents, did really exist without the mind; and for this reason it seemed needful to suppose some unthinking *substratum* or *substance* wherein they did exist, since they could not be conceived to exist by themselves. . . . (*Principles* sec. 73.)

O'Connor sees that there is *a* doctrine about substance of a purely logical kind. But he brings it in as an afterthought; dismisses it as an impossible interpretation of "the substratum theory," for no reason I can imagine except that he has taken Berkeley as his source for Locke; and shows, by his use of "something" in the first sentence, that he has not seen how distinct the two doctrines are:

It is certainly not logically necessary, or even true, that colours, for instance, cannot occur except as properties of a coloured something. If I stare at a light for a few seconds and then turn my gaze away, I shall see an "after-image" in the form of a coloured patch which certainly does not inhere in any substance. The supporter of the substratum theory of substance has either to claim (i) that the after-image is itself a substance or (ii) that it inheres in my visual field. (i) is a *reductio ad absurdum* of the substratum theory, though a sense datum would qualify as a substance in the *logical* sense of the word: it has properties without being itself a property of anything. . . .[1]

Warnock tells us that according to Locke "there is a world of physical ('external') objects" which within certain limits "actually have the qualities which our ideas incline us to assign to them."[2] Then later: "Locke had asserted the existence of 'matter,' 'material substance,' a *something* of which nothing could be either said or known."[3] Does this introduce a second Lockean doctrine? Warnock seems not to think so. Is he then pointing out a flat inconsistency in a single Lockean doctrine? Apparently not: like Berkeley before him, Warnock presents as Locke's "doctrine" something which is flatly and obviously inconsistent, yet does not call attention to this inconsistency because, one presumes, he has not noticed it. The double metaphor with which Warnock places the Lockean duplicate world "somehow behind or beneath" the world of experience reflects nicely his uncertainty as to just what view he wishes to attribute to Locke.

Ayer uses the phrase "sensible properties" in high Berkeleian fashion to effect a slide from "the thing itself as opposed to anything which may be said about it" to "the thing itself [as opposed to] its appearances":

It happens to be the case that we cannot, in our language, refer to the sensible properties of a thing without introducing a word or phrase which appears to stand for the thing itself as opposed to anything which may be said about it. And, as a result of this, those who are infected with the

---

1 D. J. O'Connor, *John Locke* (London, Penguin Books, 1952), pp. 80–1.
2 G. J. Warnock, *Berkeley* (London, Penguin Books, 1953) pp. 95–6.
3 *Ibid.*, p. 109.

primitive superstition that to every name a single real entity must correspond assume that it is necessary to distinguish logically between the thing itself and any, or all, of its sensible properties. And so they employ the term "substance" to refer to the thing itself. But from the fact that we happen to employ a single word to refer to a thing, and make that word the grammatical subject of the sentences in which we refer to the sensible appearances of the thing, it does not by any means follow that the thing itself is a "simple entity," or that it cannot be defined in terms of the totality of its appearances. It is true that in talking of "its" appearances we appear to distinguish the thing from the appearances, but that is simply an accident of linguistic usage. Logical analysis shows that what makes these "appearances" the "appearances of" the same thing is not their relationship to an entity other than themselves, but their relationship to one another.[4]

PART II

Locke distinguishes between "primary" and "secondary" qualities. A thing's primary qualities are its shape, size, spatial location, velocity, and degree of hardness; its secondary qualities are its color, temperature, smell, taste, and sound. Locke's attempt in *Essay* II, viii, 9, to give a general definition of this distinction is unsuccessful, but for present purposes the above lists suffice.

According to Locke, the secondary qualities of things are not "of" or "in" them in the same full-blooded sense as are their primary qualities. To say of something that it "is purple," for example, is to employ a natural and permissible *façon de parler;* while to say of something that it "is spherical" may be to state a plain fact in a way which requires neither gloss nor apology. I shall try to show that something true and interesting is misexpressed by this Lockean thesis, and that Berkeley's conflation of it with Locke's veil-of-perception doctrine reflects Berkeley's total failure to see what Locke was getting at in his discussion of primary and secondary qualities.

1. *The Phenol Argument.* Phenol-thio-urea tastes intensely bitter to 75 per cent of humans; to the rest it is tasteless. With a 25 per cent block of "non-tasters," we cannot say outright that the stuff is bitter: it tastes bitter to more people than not, but there is no such thing as "the" taste of it. If the non-tasters comprised only .001 per cent of all humans, then we could describe phenol-thio-urea as bitter without qualification: perhaps lemons are tasteless to .001 per cent of humans, but lemons are sour for all that. Suppose a world where phenol-thio-

⁴ A. J. Ayer, *Language, Truth and Logic* (London, Victor Gollancz, 1946), p. 42.

urea is unqualifiedly bitter, i.e., tastes so to almost everyone. Suppose further that a dynasty of world dictators begins intensive breeding of non-tasters and gradually allows the tasters to die out. After a few dozen generations, phenol-thio-urea is tasteless to everyone living, so that there are as good grounds for calling phenol-thio-urea tasteless as for calling water tasteless.

This describes a course of events in which something (a) is bitter at one time, (b) is tasteless at a later time, and (c) does not itself change in the interim. This, on the face of it, is a contradiction; and we can resolve it only by saying that the stuff's bitterness is not one of "its properties" in the full-blooded sense in which a thing's losing one of its properties *is* its changing.

Similar arguments could be developed for the taste of any given kind of stuff, and also for colors, sounds, and smells. A simple genetic control would not always be available; but mass micro-surgery might bring it about that no human could see any difference in color between grass and blood, and to do this would be to bring it about that grass was the same color as blood. Similarly for other pairs of colors, and for tastes, sounds, and smells.

We may still call things green or sour or stinking or noisy, but philosophers should bear in mind the essentially relative nature of these adjectives and their like: "similar in color" means "looking similar in color to nearly everyone under normal conditions," and a careful metaphysic will take note of that fact.

The foregoing paragraphs contain what I shall for short call "the phenol argument." Before relating it to Locke and Berkeley, I should say at once that the argument is not valid. It depends upon the epitome which says that phenol-thio-urea is bitter at one time, tasteless at a later time, *and yet does not itself change in the interim*. The italicized clause is false: in the original story phenol-thio-urea does undergo a change, namely a change in respect of its taste. Admittedly it does not change its chemical structure, but to infer from this that it does not change at all is simply to beg the question in favor of primary qualities. The story shows that a thing may change in respect of its secondary qualities without changing its primary qualities; but this is not a contrast between primary and secondary qualities, for it is also true that a thing's primary qualities may change without any change in its secondary qualities.

It is natural to protest that the phenol-thio-urea in the story, one might say, does not change in itself. I shall try below to show what justice there is in this: to see the force of such phrases as "does not change in itself" is to see what the truth is about primary and secondary qualities.

2. *Locke and Berkeley on Secondary Qualities.* The phenol argument is mine, not Locke's: he does not suggest that a secondary quality of something might be altered by a species-wide physiological change. His discussions of primary and secondary qualities in II, viii, 9–26; xxiii, 11; and IV, iii, 11–13, 28–29 strongly suggest, however, that Locke would welcome the phenol argument as making his kind of point for his kind of reason. His own detailed arguments are more obviously unsatisfactory than the phenol argument; and yet even they give to some readers the impression that there is something true here which Locke is mishandling. I shall try to show that this impression is correct; but first let us see what Locke's arguments are, and what Berkeley does with them.

(1) Locke thinks that those of our sensory states which enable us to make secondary-quality discriminations between things can be explained in terms of the things' primary qualities: seen colors, for example, can be explained in terms of surface-textures, the impact upon our eyes of particles of light, and so on. But he stresses (II, viii, 11–13; IV, iii, 12–13, 28–29) that these explanations depend upon brute-fact, non-necessary, God-ordained correlations between our secondary-quality sensory states and the primary qualities which underlie and explain them. He seems to think—though he is reticent about this—that our seeings and feelings of the primary qualities of things have a necessary connection with the primary qualities themselves; perhaps because in that case there is supposed to be not only an explanatory or causal relationship but also a resemblance (II, viii, 15). Berkeley dismisses the talk about resemblances between ideas and bodies (*Principles* sec. 9); and argues that in any case there is only brute fact observed regularity in any of the connections ordinarily taken to be causal (sec. 25, 30–31). I assume that Berkeley is right on both these points, and that if Locke has got hold of a truth about primary and secondary qualities it must be sought elsewhere.

(2) In II, viii, 20, Locke says: "Pound an almond, and the clear white colour will be altered into a dirty one, and the sweet taste into an oily one. What real alteration can the beating of the pestle make in any body, but an alteration of the texture of it?" Berkeley does not, I think, address himself directly to this; but he would have said that the beating of the pestle cannot make, or cause, any alteration whatsoever.

His reasons for this lie outside my present scope, but this argument of Locke's is itself important, as I shall show. We may notice right away that the argument begs the question: Locke invites us to say that because the pestle can cause only primary-quality changes in the almond, the secondary-quality changes must therefore be primary-quality ones in disguise; but this can be rebutted by saying that beating something with a pestle can cause alterations other than primary-quality ones, as is proved by what happens to the color and taste of an almond when it is beaten with a pestle.

(3) In II, viii, 21, Locke points out that the same water may at once feel warm to one hand and cool to the other, which "figure never does, that never producing the idea of a square by one hand which has produced the idea of a globe by the other." Berkeley concedes the point about the warm/cool water phenomenon, but claims that it has primary-quality analogues, as can be discovered "by looking with one eye bare, and with the other through a microscope" (*First Dialogue*, pp. 219–222 in the Everyman edition).

(4) In II, xxiii, 11, Locke says that to the naked eye blood looks "all red," but through a good microscope it is seen as "some few globules of red swimming in a pellucid liquor; and how these red globules would appear, if glasses could be found that could yet magnify them 1,000 or 10,000 times more, is uncertain." Again, Berkeley agrees (*First Dialogue*, pp. 214–216) but says that analogous considerations apply to size, which is a primary quality (pp. 219–220).

(5) In II, viii, 16–18, Locke says that no reason can be given for saying that the heat is "actually in the fire" which would not also be a reason for saying that the pain is actually in the fire; yet it is clearly wrong to say the latter. Berkeley agrees with this cordially (*First Dialogue*, pp. 207–209), but takes it that here again there is no difference between primary and secondary qualities.

In each of (3), (4), and (5) Locke says something about secondary qualities which he thinks will show that they sit looser to the world than is usually thought; and in each case Berkeley kidnaps Locke's remark and uses it to prise primary qualities off the world as well. Yet Locke is *wrong* in that part of each claim which Berkeley *accepts*. In (3), it does not follow—and should not even seem to follow—from the fact that we may err about temperatures that therefore things do not really have temperatures. In (4), the microscopic appearance of blood serves Locke's purpose only if it is possible that through a powerful enough microscope we should see the minute parts of blood as entirely colorless; and that is impossible since, for purposes of this argument, "colorless" must mean "invisible." In (5), it is not true that any grounds we could give for assigning temperatures to things would also be grounds for assigning pains to them.

Berkeley's view is not merely that what Locke says about secondary qualities is false unless it is so construed as to hold also for primary qualities. Berkeley genuinely agrees that things do not really have secondary qualities, and dissents only by saying that this is *also* true of primary qualities.

The explanation of this is as follows. Berkeley thinks that in agreeing with what Locke unclearly says about secondary qualities he is agreeing that a phenomenalist or idealist analysis ought to be given of statements about the secondary qualities of things, i.e., that talk about things' colors and smells and sounds, etc., is to be understood as shorthand for talk about certain sorts of sensory states. It is this thesis which he believes to hold also for talk about the primary qualities of things; it is the thesis which Berkeley offers as a rival to Locke's veil-of-perception account of the distinction between appearance and reality. Berkeley, in short, takes Locke's thesis about secondary qualities to be a *qualification* of his veil-of-perception doctrine. The latter says that there are facts about nonmental reality which are logically unconnected with facts about sensory states; and Berkeley takes the secondary-qualities doctrine to be an important rider to the effect that the genuinely extramental facts about reality are those which involve primary qualities only and do not include those which involve secondary qualities.

This account of what Berkeley is about explains the passages to which I have called attention as well as many more like them; and it is strongly confirmed by *Principles* sec. 14–15. If I am right about this, then Berkeley has completely misunderstood the kind of thing which Locke was trying to say; but I cannot justify this last claim without first saying what I think to be the truth about primary and secondary qualities.

3. *Color Blindness and Size-"Blindness."* Locke calls attention to the ways in which our perception of secondary qualities may vary according to the bodily condition of the percipient and according to the state of the percipient's environment. Berkeley rightly says that such variations also infect our perception of primary qualities but wrongly implies that the two sorts of quality are on a level in this respect. To see that they are not on a level, and why, is to grasp the truth after which Locke is fumbling.

I shall contrast two kinds of sensory aberration: in one, someone sees two things as being of the same color when in fact they are not, and in the other someone sees and feels two things as being of the same size when in fact they are not.

Suppose, then, that someone who is confronted by a red thing and a white thing convinces us that he sees them as having exactly the same color. He may believe us when we tell him that the things do have different colors; and if they differ in no other way we can, without asking him to trust us, prove to him that there is some difference between the two things which we see and he does not. Also, we may show him—or he may discover for himself—that the two objects differ in respect of the wave lengths of the light they reflect, and that wave lengths usually correlate with seen colors. But if he ignores other people's talk about the two objects, and ignores esoteric facts of optics, he may never discover that his seeing of the two objects as having the same color arises from a sensory defect in him. A failure of secondary-quality discrimination, in one who is otherwise sensorily normal, can—and sometimes does—persist unsuspected through any variations in distance or angle of view, light-conditions, mouth-washing, cold-curing, and so on.

Contrast this with the case of a size-"blind" man who, going by what he sees and feels, judges a certain drinking mug to have the same size as a certain cup, although in fact the former is both higher and wider than the latter. In such a case, we can place the cup inside the mug; or fill the mug with water, and then fill the cup from the mug and pour the remaining water on the ground; or place both vessels on a horizontal surface and draw the size-"blind" man's hand across the top of the cup until it is stopped by the side of the mug; and so on. What are we to suppose happens when our size-"blind" man is confronted by these manipulations of the cup and the mug? There are just two relevant possibilities. (a) We may suppose that the size-"blind" man has a normal apprehension of what happens when we manipulate the cup and the mug, and therefore quite soon realizes that his original judgment about their sizes must have been mistaken. (b) We may suppose that in each case there is some supplementary inadequacy in his perception of what is done to the cup and the mug, or the outcome of what is done, so that what he sees and feels still fits in smoothly with his original judgment that the two vessels are of the same size.

To adopt supposition (a) is just to admit that this case is radically different from that of color blindness. If the point of the latter were just that there are or could be aberrations in our perception of secondary qualities, then we could say the same of primary qualities. What gives relevance and bite to color blindness, and to abnormality of secondary-quality perception generally, is the fact that any such abnormality can persist, not just for a few moments or under special conditions, without the victim's being given any clue to his abnormality by his other, normal sensory responses.

If we want an analogy between size-"blindness" and color blindness, then, we must adopt supposition (b). But look at what this involves: the size-"blind" man must be unable to see or feel that the cup is inside the mug, or unable to see or feel that the mug has not momentarily stretched or the cup contracted; he must be unable to see or feel that the cup has been filled from the mug, or unable to see or feel that there is water left in the mug after the cup has been filled; he must be unable to see or feel that his hand is touching the cup as it moves across the top of it, or unable to see or feel his hand being stopped by the side of the mug.

This is bad enough, but there is worse to follow. If the size-"blind" man is to be unable to see or feel the water which remains in the mug after the cup has been filled from it, this will require yet further sensory aberrations on his part: if the water is poured over a lighted candle, or used to dissolve a lump of sugar, or thrown in the size-"blind" man's face, his perception of any of these events must also be appropriately abnormal if his original judgment is to remain unchallenged. Similarly with any of the other sensory aberrations with which we must prop up the initial one: each requres further props which demand yet others in their turn, and so on indefinitely.

The desired analogy with color blindness has collapsed yet again. In the case of color blindness, the sensory abnormality was not clued by the victim's other sensory responses although these were normal; but to keep the size-"blind" man in ignorance of his own initial sensory abnormality we have had to surround it with ever-widening circles of further abnormalities.

Strictly speaking, it is not quite correct to say that the single failure of color-discrimination could well remain unclued by the victim's other, normal sensory responses: we must suppose our man to be unable to see color differences between red things and white things generally. This, however, does not restore the analogy. For the infectious spread of sensory aberrations around the single initial failure of size-discrimination does not involve merely other failures to discriminate sizes, but must also involve failures of shape-discrimination, movement-detection, sensitivity to heat, and so on. The single red/white failure spreads to red/white failures generally, but need spread no further.

As well as losing our analogy, we are also losing our grip on the initial datum of the size-"blindness" case, namely that we can agree with the size-"blind" man about the identity of a certain cup and mug, disagreeing with him only about their relative sizes. For it has turned out that there are countless visible and tangible aspects of our environment in regard to which the size-"blind" man does not agree with us, so that it is now by no means clear that we can still assume that we share with him a sensory awareness of a single objective world.

4. *The Crucial Contrasts.* The foregoing discussion of color blindness and size-"blindness" illustrates two crucial and closely related contrasts between primary and secondary qualities.

(1) There are countless familiar, exoteric, general facts about the connections between a thing's primary qualities and its ways of interacting with other things: a rigid thing cannot be enclosed within a smaller rigid thing; a thing cannot block another thing's fall to the earth without touching it; a cube cannot roll smoothly on a flat surface; a thing's imprint on soft wax matches the outline of the thing itself; and so on, indefinitely. The analogue of this does not hold for secondary qualities. Admittedly, there are connections between a thing's color, say, and its ways of behaving in relation to other things: in general, a brown apple will be more squashable than a green one; a blue flame will boil a pint of water faster than a yellow flame of the same size; a thing's color will correlate with the wave lengths of the light it reflects: and so on. But neither for colors nor for any other secondary qualities can we make, as we can for primary qualities, an enormously long list of obvious, familiar, inescapable connections of the relevant kind.

(2) Just because of the numerousness and familiarity of the connections between the primary qualities of things and their ways of interacting with one another, no clear sense attaches to the suggestion that something might persistently fail to obey these general connections. If a thing's purported size is belied by enough of its ways of interacting with other things, there is no point in saying that it does have that size. As against this, there would be a point in saying that a thing was red even if this were belied by the wave lengths of the light reflected from its surface, or by its flavor, hardness, chemical composition, etc. If in sunlight a given thing were indistinguishable in color

from other things which were agreed to be red, then this fact could sensibly enough be reported in the words "That thing is red," even if we had to add one or more riders such as ". . . though its light-reflecting properties are atypical for red," or ". . . though its taste is atypical for red wine," or ". . . though its temperature is atypical for red iron." There is in fact a tight correlation between wave lengths of reflected light and the colors seen by most people in sunlight, and we therefore do not have to decide either for or against defining color-words in terms of how things look and treating the associated wave lengths as mere empirical correlates of colors. If the need for a decision did arise, however, we could choose to give our color terminology a purely visual basis and still have it doing pretty much the work which it does for us now. Analogous remarks apply also to all other secondary qualities. Not so, however, for primary qualities. As the discussion of size-"blindness" showed, the interrelations between things in respect of their primary qualities are numerous and various and tightly interlocked. There seems to be little chance of inventing a partial breakdown of them such that those which survive the breakdown could form a basis for a working vocabulary of primary qualities.

   We can now see why the phenol argument is plausible, and why it really does show something about secondary qualities as against primary. We know what it would be like to be aware that the taste of phenol-thio-urea had been altered by means of a change of the human frame. But what could ever entitle us to say "Oranges, which used to be spherical, are now cubic; but this change has been brought about solely by a change in humans"? The difficulty here is not merely our ignorance of appropriate surgical or eugenic techniques, nor the scientific implausibility of suggesting that such techniques might be discovered: if the obstacles were only of that sort, then it would be historically impossible that the point brought out by the phenol argument should be one of which Locke was dimly aware. The trouble we meet in trying to reproduce a primary-quality analogue of the phenol argument is that we must either (a) allow the analogy to fail by supposing only that erstwhile spheres "look cubic" in some very restricted sense, e.g., in the sense of presenting visual fields like those now presented by sugar cubes when seen at rest (while in all other ways looking and feeling spherical); or (b) allow the analogy to fail by telling an astronomically complicated story in which not only the shapes of erstwhile spheres but also thousands of other aspects of the world were perceived differently; or (c) insulate shape from its present correlates by means of some radical conceptual revision which has no analogue in the phenol argument and which no one can see how to perform anyway. Of these alternatives, (a) and (b) do not produce the desired analogy, and perhaps (c) does not either; while (b) and (c) involve conceptual and empirical complications which we have no idea how to handle.

This difference between primary and secondary qualities is closely connected with the fact that the former alone involve the sense of touch. How they involve it, and what this has to do with the contrast I have drawn, are matters which I cannot go into here.

5. *The Relevance of This to Locke.* Locke says nothing about color blindness: it seems not to have been generally recognized in his day. Yet I maintain that the contrast I have drawn between primary and secondary qualities, and which I have approached through a discussion of sensory abnormalities, is one which Locke saw dimly and was struggling to express and defend. My grounds for this contention are the following.

(1) The points which I have made could without absurdity be summed up in the Lockean remark that it is true of secondary qualities, in a way in which it is not of primary, that they are "merely" the powers which things have to affect us in certain ways.

(2) Locke was aware that primary qualities are all logically connected with solidity and extension and these he regarded as definitive of "body" (II, iv, 1–2). Furthermore, he thought that the essentialness of "solid" and "extended" to "body" was connected with the different ways in which primary and secondary qualities are qualities "of" bodies, though he seems to have misunderstood the nature of the connection (II, viii, 9). My discussion indicates that Locke is right about the definition of "body," and right in his assumption that this is a deep conceptual fact which is not on a par with the dictionary definition of "brother" as "male sibling."

(3) Part of Locke's thesis about primary and secondary qualities is that if we knew enough we could give causal explanations, purely in primary-quality terms, for all our secondary-quality discriminations. Over the possibility of a purely primary-quality science, Locke had an optimism which was not at all justified by the state of physiology in the seventeenth century: note his calm assumption that *of course* the pestle's effect on the almond must be describable purely in primary-quality terms. My discussion of primary qualities shows why someone

in Locke's position should so confidently assume that the final, perfect science will require only a primary-quality vocabulary.

(4) Several of Locke's examples share with the phenol example an emphasis upon the notion of a thing's changing in respect of a secondary quality without changing *in itself*. When Locke said that porphyry in the dark has no color, he erred; but he seems clearly to have had in mind the fact that our main basis—he would have said our only basis—for attributing colors to things is such that our color-reports can vary without any change in the things themselves. My discussion shows why this is plausible and how far it is true.

6. *Berkeley's Blunder.* I submit, then, that I have presented a truth about primary and secondary qualities and that it is this after which Locke was groping. Now, the point which I have brought out has nothing to do with the veil-of-perception doctrine: it is not a version of that doctrine, or a qualification of or a rival to it. It operates on a different level altogether. One can state and explain what is interesting in the distinction between primary and secondary qualities —whether or not one goes so far as to say that secondary qualities are not "of" things as primary qualities are—only on the basis of normal assumptions about our entitlement to trust the evidence of our senses. What I have called Locke's "veil-of-perception doctrine" is really just his mishandling of a certain sceptical question, and the latter makes sense only if it asks whether the objective world is, really, *in any way at all* as it appears to be. An affirmative answer must be given to this question before one can present the contrast between primary and secondary qualities.

The thesis about primary and secondary qualities can be taken as a qualification of the veil-of-perception doctrine only in the following extremely minimal way. The veil-of-perception doctrine says that statements about objects are logically dissociated from statements about states of mind, and the primary/secondary thesis can be seen as conceding that this logical dissociation does not hold for statements attributing secondary qualities to objects but only for those attributing primary qualities to them. I think that it is because the relation between the two doctrines can be viewed like this that they are so often conflated; and it is therefore important to see what is wrong with this way of looking at the matter.

Considered as a qualification of the veil-of-perception doctrine, i.e., as a concession that not all statements about objects are logically dissociated from statements about states of mind, the primary/secondary thesis is just a bore. Even the most fervent super-Lockean would agree that some predicates of objects are connected with mental predicates; for example, that we commit ourselves to something about states of mind when we say that castor oil is nasty, or that the New York subway system is confusing. What makes Locke's thesis about secondary qualities interesting is not its saying (a) "Some predicates of objects have *some* logical connections with mental predicates," but rather its saying (b) "Secondary-quality predicates of objects have *these* logical connections with mental predicates." Now (b) does not offer any useful support to the view that there are logical connections between all predicates of objects and mental predicates: the Lockean view of the status of secondary qualities is no more a stage on the way to complete idealism or phenomenalism than is the Nazi valuation of Aryans a stage on the way to a belief in the worth and dignity of all men. In each case, the further step may consistently be taken; but in neither case is the taking of it just a further development of the line of thought by which the first stage was reached.

Just as the Lockean thesis about secondary qualities is not a significant *restriction* on the veil-of-perception doctrine, so the Lockean thesis about primary qualities is not—or need not be—a somewhat restricted *version* of the veil-of-perception doctrine. If to (a) "Some predicates of objects have *some* logical connections with mental predicates" we add the rider "but primary-quality predicates don't," then the result is indeed all of a piece with the veil-of-perception doctrine, and is thus in opposition to idealism or phenomenalism. But if to (b) "Secondary-quality predicates of objects have *these* logical connections with mental predicates" we add the rider "but primary qualities don't," the result says only that primary-quality predicates are not connected with mental predicates *in the way in which* secondary-quality predicates are. This presents no challenge at all to Berkeley or to any phenomenalist who knows what he is about.

This difference of level between the two theses is fairly clear in Locke's own pages. In his battles with the sceptic, Locke does invoke empirical facts which are not legitimately available to him; but he does this covertly, and knows that he ought not to do it at all: As against this, his discussions of the primary/secondary contrast are riddled with open appeals to experimental evidence. (This is perfectly proper: a satisfactory treatment of the primary/secondary distinction must begin with empirical facts; though it ought, as Locke's does not, to connect these with the relevant conceptual points.) Locke notes this explicitly in II, viii, 22: "I have, in what just goes before, been engaged in physical inquiries a little farther than perhaps I intended. . . . I hope I shall be pardoned this little excursion into natural philosophy, it being necessary, in our present inquiry, to distinguish the primary and real qualities of bodies, which are always in them . . . etc." Again, in IV, iii, 28, he denies that any "correspondence or connexion" can be found between our ideas of secondary qualities "and those primary qualities which (experience shows us) produce them in us." In the context of the battle against the sceptic, these references to "physical inquiries" and to what "experience shows us" would be merely grotesque. Still less do we find Locke mixing up the primary/secondary thesis with the question of substratum-substance. In his principal exposition of the former, II, viii, 9–26, the word "substance" does not occur.

I conclude, then, that some things worth saying about the primary/secondary distinction are pointed to by Locke's discussion of it, and have no clear logical connection with the philosophical problem about the distinction between what appears to be the case and what is really the case.

It is for his insights into the latter problem that Berkeley is chiefly valued: he is rightly seen as a precursor of phenomenalism, and even those who hold no brief for phenomenalism agree that Berkeley taught us much about what goes wrong when the distinction between appearance and reality is divorced, as it is by Locke, from anything cashable in experience. But if we are to understand what is happening in Berkeley's pages, we must see through his appalling conflation of the question about the appearance/reality distinction with both the question about substance and that about the primary/secondary distinction. Consider for example the following passage from *Principles* sec. 9:

. . . they will have our ideas of the primary qualities to be patterns or images of things which exist without the mind, in an unthinking substance they call *matter*. By matter, therefore, we are to understand an inert, senseless substance, in which extension, figure, motion and so forth do actually subsist, but it is evident from what we have already shown that extension, figure and motion are only ideas existing in the mind, and that an idea can be like nothing but another idea, and that consequently neither they nor their archetypes can exist in an unperceiving substance. Hence it is plain, that the very notion of what is called *matter*, or *corporeal substance*, involves a contradiction in it.

How could anyone spell out in plain terms what it is that is being opposed here, except on the basis of an elaborate exposure of the two conflations? Many passages in *Principles* and *Three Dialogues* are similarly unintelligible until the two conflations have been understood and rejected; and Berkeley's writings are full of tensions which can be resolved only on that same basis. For example, according to the primary/secondary doctrine, things do have primary qualities in a way in which they do not have secondary; according to the veil-of-perception doctrine things may really have none of the properties we attribute to them; and of course substratum-substances cannot have, *qua* substances, any properties at all. And so, although "by matter, therefore, we are to understand an inert, senseless substance, in which extension, figure, motion and so forth do actually subsist," *Principles* sec. 47 tells us that "the matter philosophers contend for is an incomprehensible somewhat, which hath none of those particular qualities whereby the bodies falling under our senses are distinguished one from another."

The literature does not yield the same rich harvest of examples of this conflation as it does for the one discussed in the first part of my paper. Most commentators merely take Berkeley's word for it that the veil-of-perception doctrine is integrally connected with the thesis about primary and secondary qualities, and lurch somehow across the gap where the connection is supposed to be. In somewhat the same way, they accept without argument Berkeley's demonstrably false claim that Locke's theory of abstract ideas is connected with the three-headed monster which Berkeley calls Locke's doctrine of material substance.

University of Cambridge.

THE EXISTENCE OF GOD

BERKELEY AND GOD*

Jonathan Bennett

It is well known that Berkeley had two arguments for the existence of
God. A while ago, in trying to discover what these arguments are and
how they fit into Berkeley's scheme of things, I encountered certain
problems which I think that I have now solved. In this paper I present
my results.

THE CONTINUITY ARGUMENT

The argument which is immortalised in the limericks about the
tree in the quad, and which I shall call the continuity argument, goes as
follows:

    (a) No idea, and therefore no collection of ideas, can exist when not
        perceived by some spirit;

    (b) Objects are collections of ideas, and therefore cannot exist when
        not perceived by some spirit;

    (c) Objects do sometimes exist when not perceived by any human
        spirit;

therefore

    (d) There must be one or more non-human spirits which perceive
        objects when no human spirit perceives them.

The first premiss reflects Berkeley's penchant for speaking of
ideas which people "perceive" where one would prefer that he spoke of
sensory states which people may be in; but that raises issues which go
too deep to be explored now. The second premiss reflects Berkeley's
failure to see that, even if what we say about objects is reducible to
what we say about sensory states, the mode of reduction might be too
complex for terms like "collection" to be in place; but that too lies
deep in Berkeley's thought and forms no part of my present concern.
Nor shall I consider the yawning gulf between the conclusion of the
argument and the Christian monotheism which it is supposed to serve.
The questions which I do wish to answer are these:

* From *Philosophy*, XL (1965), 207–21. Reprinted by permission of the
author and the editors of *Philosophy*.

146

(1) Why does Berkeley think that he is entitled to the argument's third premiss, which says that objects do exist when not perceived by any human spirit? The argument depends, through its second premiss, upon equating statements about the existence of objects not with statements about sensory states which *would* be had if certain conditions obtained, but with statements about the existence of sensory states the having of which is the perceiving of objects. From this, one would have thought, it follows very obviously that there could not be grounds for saying that any object exists at a time when no human perceives it.

(2) Why does Berkeley not use the continuity argument in his *Principles of Human Knowledge?* It will not do to say that he did not think of it until after that work was written, and that this is why it appears only in the *Three Dialogues.* If Berkeley had seen how bad the argument is, he would not have used it at all; failing to see that, he ought to have thought it deeply satisfactory. If, in addition, the continuity argument came to him as a new discovery after the writing of the *Principles,* he would surely have highlighted it in the later work which was supposed to remedy the unfavourable reception of the earlier. Yet in the *Three Dialogues* the argument is presented just once, in a passage consisting of two short sentences. This remark may be found surprising, but I shall justify it.

THE PASSIVITY ARGUMENT

Berkeley's other argument for God's existence, which I shall call the passivity argument, goes as follows:

(a) My ideas of sense (i.e. those which I have when I perceive objective states of affairs) come into my mind without being caused to do so by any act of my will;

(b) The occurrence of any idea must be caused by the will of some being in whose mind the idea occurs;

therefore

(c) My ideas of sense are in the mind of, and caused by the will of, some being other than myself.

Underlying this argument is Berkeley's belief that the only genuinely causal activity is the purposeful behaviour of sentient beings. The argument also involves a dubious assumption about the notion of an "act of the will." These flaws in the argument go to the heart of some of Berkeley's most radical errors, but I shall discuss neither them nor the extent to which the conclusion falls short of Christianity. The questions which I wish to answer are these:

(3) Why does Berkeley accept the second premiss of the argument? Granted his belief that causal activity is the prerogative of "the will of a spirit," why does Berkeley think that every change in anyone's sensory state must have a cause?

(4) Does Berkeley see—and, if so, why does he not *say*—that the passivity argument gives to God a quite different scope from that given to him by the continuity argument? By the passivity argument, God perceives objects when we perceive them; by the continuity argument, God perceives objects when we do not. The two arguments are agreeably complementary. Why does Berkeley not call attention to this striking feature of his theological arguments?

THE POINT OF THE QUESTIONS

I have waived a number of objections which depend upon Berkeley's not having seen further than he did into the nature of objectivity concepts, causal necessity, volition, sensory states, and so on. He was only Berkeley, not God; it takes time, and generations of stumbling, to get these deep and difficult matters right. But my question (1) does not concern a deep error on Berkeley's part, but simply points to an obvious conflict between the continuity argument and one of Berkeley's most cherished views. We must therefore answer the question if we are able to trace the movement of thought in Berkeley's pages. To understand a philosopher we need not believe everything he says, but we must at least be able to see how he could have made the mistakes which he did make. My answers to questions (2) and (4) will, it is true, rob (1) of most of its interest; but it is nevertheless just worth asking, and there are exegetical lessons to be learned from answering it.

My question (3), about the assumption that every change of sensory state is caused, is in a slightly different case. It is arguable that Berkeley was one of those philosophers—we know there have been many—who assume without question that there are no absolutely brute facts. I found this answer to (3) unconvincing, even before I had an alternative to it; and there *is* an alternative. Berkeley may not have taken it as axiomatic that every change of sensory state must be caused: he does give a reason for accepting this premiss of the passivity argument. I have found it only once in Berkeley's writings, and it may be that Berkeley put no weight upon it, and was after all one of those for whom it is axiomatic that every "Why?"-question has an answer. Nevertheless, as with (1), there is profit to be gained from taking question (3) as seriously as possible, if only because (1) and (3) are useful pegs on which to hang some exegetical material which is vital for the answering of (2) and (4).

Questions (2) and (4) raise general issues about what sort of thing Berkeley thought he was doing with his theological arguments and—more important—*what kind of scepticism it was that he was so anxious to disavow*. Unless these issues are resolved, we cannot have an intelligent and informed picture of what is happening in the *Principles* and the *Three Dialogues*.

There is another matter which concerns all four questions. Berkeley's thought has more hard, complex structure than is usually realised. In his pages there is a less elaborate apparatus of self-conscious pros and cons, explanations and caveats, definitions and distinctions, than we should expect to find in a twentieth-century writer of similar scope; but the complexity and intellectual sophistication are there all the same; and it seems to me bad and unhealthy that Berkeley should be kept alive, to be hurriedly scanned from time to time and made the subject of elementary books, without proper attention being paid to the detailed ways in which his thought moved.

AN ANSWER TO QUESTION (3)

The question is: Why does Berkeley, in the passivity argument, help himself to the assumption that there must be what he would call a "cause" for any change in anyone's sensory state? In *Principles* sec. 26 he says: "We perceive a continual succession of ideas, some are anew excited, others are changed or disappear. There is therefore some cause of these ideas whereon they depend, and which produces and changes them." This suggests that Berkeley just is a philosopher of that familiar kind who cannot entertain the possibility that an intelligible "Why?" might have no answer. This broadly rationalist frame of mind is sympathetically described by Warnock when he answers question (3) thus: "The true foundation of his view is, I believe, the conviction that to hold that events merely *occur*, without any purpose and volition behind them or anything analogous with purpose and volition, is to say

something which is really quite *unintelligible. . . ."* (*Berkeley,*
p. 123). Consider *Principles* sec. 29: "Whatever power I may have
over my own thoughts, I find the ideas actually perceived by sense
have not a like dependence on my will. . . . There is therefore some
other will or spirit that produces them. . . ." This looks like support
for Warnock's diagnosis of him as, in a broad sense, a rationalist.

On the other hand, Berkeley does not read like a rationalist. In
his account of those regularities which are usually taken to be causal,
he is as blandly and confidently final as Hume, and one does not have
the impression that this is only because he thinks that in disqualifying
observed regularities from counting as causal he is making room for
something else equally comprehensive. This is a matter of tone and of
nuance, and unaided it will bear no weight at all; but it is confirmed in
Principles sec. 146: "Those things which are called the works of
nature, that is, the far greater part of the ideas or sensations perceived
by us, are not produced by, or dependent on, the wills of men. There
is therefore some other spirit that causes them, since it is repugnant
that they should subsist by themselves." Here Berkeley gives a *reason*
for saying that a change in my ideas which I do not cause must be
caused by some other spirit, namely that ideas cannot "subsist by
themselves." Normally, when Berkeley says that ideas cannot subsist
by themselves, he is making a point about the ownership of ideas:
every idea must be someone's. But now, it seems, he is inferring from
this that the occurrence of any idea must be caused. This is a non-
sequitur, but there is a distinction to be made between a thesis which a
philosopher defends by an invalid argument and one which he sees no
need to support with arguments at all.

There is something to be learned from this particular non-
sequitur. I think that it turns upon an ambiguity in the word "depend": I suggest, that is, that in the passage I have quoted Berkeley
slides from "not dependent on (= not caused by) my mind" to
"dependent on (= caused by) some other mind," through the general
formula that necessarily every idea must depend on (= exist in, or be
owned by) some mind.

It is certainly true that when Berkeley discusses the relation
between ideas and minds in terms of "depend" and its grammatical
cognates, he does use these words both to talk about the ownership of
ideas by minds and to talk about the causing of ideas by minds. The
facts are as follows. There is a muddled and unclassifiable use of
"dependent" in *Principles* sec. 12; there are half a dozen places where

"depend" is used logically, i.e. where a theory is said to depend upon another theory, or a problem to depend upon a prejudice: and there are a dozen uses of "depend" or its cognates in which the items whose dependence is spoken of are not ideas at all, e.g. where Berkeley says that we depend on God or that God is independent of everything. Of the remaining uses of "depend," etc., all but four fall squarely into one or other of two classes:

The ownership uses. In *Principles* sec. 6, 89, 91, in the first dialogue, pp. 158,[1] 163–4, in the second dialogue, p. 176, and in the third dialogue, p. 223, Berkeley uses "independent," "dependent" (once) and "independency" (once) to make a point about the owner-ship of ideas. In each of these passages, the question of whether an idea is independent of a given mind is the question of whether it exists unowned by, not had by, or as Berkeley would say "not perceived by," the mind in question.

The causal uses. In *Principles* sec. 10, 26, 29, 33, 106, in the first dialogue, pp. 159–60, 169, 177, in the second dialogue, p. 179, and in the third dialogue, p. 197, Berkeley uses "depend" and four of its grammatical cognates to make a point about the *causes* of ideas. In these passages, an idea is dependent on a given mind if it is caused or "excited" by that mind.

Berkeley has, then, two distinct jobs for the "depend" family to do; and he too must agree that they *are* distinct, since he does not think that the only ideas which occur in my mind are ones which are caused by my mind. Since he nowhere comments on this double use of "depend," one suspects that he has not noticed it; and this suspicion is strengthened by *Principles* sec. 56 where Berkeley criticises an infer-ence which turns upon the very ambiguity which I have noted (the italics are mine): "Men knowing they perceived several ideas whereof they were not themselves the authors, as not being excited from within nor *depending on* the operation of their wills, this made them maintain those ideas or objects of perception had an existence *independent of* and without the mind, without ever dreaming that a contradiction was involved in those words." Here Berkeley says that a contradictory conclusion has been drawn from a true premiss, and thus he implies that the argument is invalid. Its invalidity clearly turns upon the fact

[1] Page numbers are those in D. M. Armstrong (ed.), *Berkeley's Philosophi-cal Writings* (New York, 1965). Those who do not have this volume may be helped to check my references by the information that in it the first dialogue is on pp. 135–71, the second on pp. 171–89, and the third on pp. 189–225.

that in the premiss "not . . . depending on" means "not caused by," while in the conclusion "independent of" means "not owned by"; *but Berkeley does not remark on this ambiguity.*

It therefore seems clear that the passage I have quoted from *Principles* sec. 146 should be interpreted in the way I have suggested, i.e. as an unrecognised exploitation of the ambiguity of "dependent on." At any rate, Berkeley does argue from "All ideas are owned" to "All ideas are caused." If the word "dependent" is not the source of the trouble, then the non-sequitur is about twice as bad as anything else in the book.

THE ANSWER TO QUESTION (1)

Why does Berkeley, in the continuity argument, allow himself the premiss that objects exist while not perceived by any human? A possible answer is that this is such a deep-rooted, normal human assumption that Berkeley could not help making it even though he could not, on his own philosophical principles, be entitled to make it. Thus Warnock: "Berkeley . . . knows that any plain man would insist that the furniture in an unoccupied room actually does exist, not merely that it would exist if the room were occupied; and he himself thinks that it would be merely absurd to question this" (*Berkeley*, p. 115).

This strikes me as false. In many places, Berkeley calmly says that if we clear our minds we shall see that we have no grounds for believing in the existence of objects while they are unperceived. See for example *Principles* sec. 4, and also the following from *Principles* sec. 6: "All those bodies which compose the mighty frame of the world have not any subsistence without a mind; their being (esse) is to be perceived; consequently so long as they are not actually perceived by me, or do not exist in my mind or that of any other created spirit, they must either have no existence at all, or else subsist in the mind of some eternal spirit." These are not the words of someone who would add that since objects do exist when not perceived by created spirits therefore there must be an eternal spirit which perceives them. The suggestion is rather that unless we can find independent grounds for believing that there is an eternal spirit we are not entitled to say that objects exist while not perceived by any created spirit; and someone whose mind is working this way cannot base the continuity argument for God's existence on the premiss that it is just obvious that objects exist when not perceived by any created spirit.

Again, in *Principles* sec. 45–8, Berkeley discusses the charge "that from the foregoing principles it follows [that] things are every moment annihilated and created anew. . . . Upon shutting my eyes, all the furniture in the room is reduced to nothing, and barely upon opening them it is again created." He does not reply that of course *that* would be absurd, but. . . . On the contrary, he says that the charge itself is absurd, and that, since anyone who brings it must admit that it is impossible "either for his ideas or their archetypes to exist without being perceived . . . it is unreasonable for him to stand up in defence of he knows not what, and pretend to charge on me as an absurdity the not assenting to those propositions which at bottom have no meaning" (sec. 45). He proceeds to devote two sections to arguing that certain rival schools of philosophy are committed to the same conclusion, and only then does he remark mildly that after all he is not committed to the conclusion himself: "Though we hold, indeed, the objects of sense to be nothing else but ideas which cannot exist unperceived, yet we may not hence conclude they have no existence except only while they are perceived by us, since there may be some other spirit that perceives them, though we do not. Wherever bodies are said to have no existence without the mind, I would not be understood to mean this or that particular mind, but all minds whatsoever. It does not therefore follow from the foregoing principles that bodies are annihilated and created every moment, or exist not at all during the intervals between our perception of them" (sec. 48). The crucial expressions are "we may not thence *conclude*," "there *may* be some other spirit," "it does not therefore *follow*." These are not the words of someone who proposes to base the continuity argument on the absurdity of denying that objects have a continuous existence.

We find the solution to the puzzle in the third dialogue (p. 193), where Hylas asks: "Supposing you were annihilated, cannot you conceive it possible that things perceivable by sense may still exist?" Philonous replies: "I can; but then it must be in another mind. When I deny sensible things an existence out of the mind, I do not mean my mind in particular, but all minds. Now it is plain they have an existence exterior to my mind, since I find them by experience to be independent of it. There is therefore some other mind wherein they exist, during the intervals between the time of my perceiving them: as likewise they did before my birth, and would do after my supposed annihilation." Here we have the ambiguity of "depend" etc., which I noted earlier, but this time exploited in reverse. I find "by experience" that some ideas are independent of (= not caused by) my mind, and I therefore conclude that they are independent of my mind (= owned by some mind other than mine), and thence that they can exist after my annihilation.

The passivity argument has the dubious premiss that *all ideas are caused by some mind*, while the continuity argument has the dubious premiss that *some ideas are not owned by my mind*. Now if we replace "caused" by "owned" in the former of these, the result is something which Berkeley is entitled to accept; and similarly if we replace "owned" by "caused" in the latter. Berkeley has, in effect, performed these substitutions by expressing each premiss in terms of "dependent on" and interpreting this in the way most favourable to the purpose in hand. If this is not a correct account of this third-dialogue passage, what other explanation can be given for Berkeley's allowing himself to say that we "find by experience" that some of our ideas are "exterior" to our minds in a sense which is relevant to their continuity "during the intervals between the time of our perceiving them"?

It may be thought that I have rested too much on one brief and rather casual presentation of the continuity argument; but I make no apology for this, since the passage I have quoted from the third dialogue is Berkeley's *only* presentation of the continuity argument. In my next two sections I shall show that this is so.

"REALITY" IN BERKELEY

When Berkeley talks about the "reality" of things, and about "scepticism" in that connection, he is not talking about continuity or about anything which is relevant to the continuity argument. In *Principles* sec. 33 he says: "The ideas imprinted on the senses by the author of nature are called *real things*. . . . The ideas of sense are allowed to have more reality in them, that is, to be more strong, orderly and coherent than the creatures of the mind. . . . They are also less dependent on the spirit or thinking substance which perceives them, in that they are excited by the will of another and more powerful spirit. . . ." This all concerns ideas which exist *although not caused by me*, and has nothing to do with ideas which exist *when not perceived by me*.

In *Principles* sec. 34 Berkeley faces squarely the accusation that his principles lead to scepticism about the reality of things: "It will be

objected that by the foregoing principles, all that is real and substantial
in nature is banished out of the world. . . . All things that exist, exist
only in the mind, that is, they are purely notional. What therefore
. . . must we think of houses, rivers, mountains, trees, stones . . .?
Are all these but so many chimeras and illusions on the fancy? To all
which . . . I answer that by the principles premised we are not
deprived of any one thing in nature. Whatever we see, feel, hear, or
any wise conceive or understand, remains as secure as ever, and is as
real as ever. There is a *rerum natura*, and the distinction between
realities and chimeras retains its full force. This is evident from
sections 29, 30 and 33, where we have shown what is meant by *real
things* in opposition to *chimeras*, or ideas of our own framing. . . ."
Here again there is not a word about the existence of things while they
are not perceived by me, or by any created spirit: the question of
reality is explicitly referred back to the earlier discussion which, like
the replay of it in sec. 36, is conducted solely in terms of one's
passivity in respect of ideas which one does have. Throughout sec.
30–44, Berkeley treats of reality, chimeras, scepticism, etc., entirely in
terms of ideas which one does have, and thus positively excludes the
question of continuity.

This latter question is, as we have seen, raised in sec. 45–8, where
the issue is clearly stated in terms of what can be the case at a time
when I have no ideas in my mind. Berkeley explicitly treats this as a
new question, over and above the issues about "reality" which he has
been discussing for some pages.

When in *Principles* sec. 82–4 Berkeley defends himself against
the charge that he has so emptied out the universe as to be in conflict
with holy writ, he deals with this entirely in terms of the real/imag-
inary dichotomy, and the matters of passivity on which it depends.
There is again nothing about objects existing when not perceived by
created spirits.

Finally, in *Principles* sec. 90 Berkeley talks about externality:
"The things perceived by sense may be termed external, with regard to
their origin, in that they are not generated from within by the mind
itself, but imprinted by a spirit distinct from that which perceives
them. Sensible objects may likewise be said to be without the mind in
another sense, namely when they exist in some other mind. Thus when
I shut my eyes, the things I saw may still exist, but it must be in
another mind." Berkeley calls this *another* sense of "external": so far
from running the two together, he explicitly distinguishes them.

Notice also his conspicuous failure to base any argument on the second sense of "external": he says only that the things I saw *may* still exist, but it must be in another mind. This uncombative remark fits in with Berkeley's other treatments of the question about whether any ideas or sensible things exist when I do not perceive them. I showed in my preceding section that, so far from insisting that it would be absurd to deny sensible things a continuous existence, Berkeley normally contents himself with saying mildly that he is not positively committed to any such denial. It begins to look as if, as well as distinguishing "reality" from continuity, we must also say that Berkeley cares deeply about the former but that the latter is not for him a matter of urgency or anxiety or even much interest. If this is true, as I believe it is, the implications for Berkeley's theological arguments are obvious.

THE "FALSE IMAGINARY GLARE" PASSAGE

To prove Berkeley's unconcern with the question of continuity, I need to cite all the passages in which he raises the question of things existing when not perceived by humans and show that in none of them (apart from the two-sentence continuity argument in the third dialogue) does he show any inclination to insist on the continuity of sensible things or to argue from their continuity to the existence of God. I have in fact already dealt with all Berkeley's discussions of continuity in the *Principles* and *Dialogues;* but the second dialogue contains one passage which is sometimes adduced as a source for the continuity argument. It occurs on pp. 173 ff., where Philonous sings the praises of the universe, and asks: "How should those principles be entertained that lead us to think all the visible beauty of the creation a false imaginary glare?" Hylas, who has been converted to what he takes to be Berkeley's principles, meets this with the forlorn remark that "My comfort is, you are as much a sceptic as I am"; to which Philonous replies that on the contrary *he* is not a sceptic, that scepticism does not follow from his principles and indeed is not true, and that God will come to the rescue. "As sure . . . as the sensible world really exists, so sure is there an infinite, omnipresent Spirit who contains and supports it." He also distinguishes his position from the pious declaration that God sees all: "Is there no difference between saying *there is a God, therefore he perceives all things:* and saying *sensible things do really exist: and if they really exist they are necessarily perceived by an infinite mind: therefore there is an infinite mind, or God.* This furnishes you with a direct and immediate

demonstration, from a most evident principle, of the being of a God."
This has been taken as an exposition of the continuity argument, but it
is no such thing.

Firstly, there is as I have already pointed out a sharp separation in
Berkeley between the question of whether things "exist when not
perceived by human minds" and the question of whether anything "is
real," "really exists," "is not imaginary," etc., these latter expressions
being elucidated by Berkeley mainly in terms of the *causes* of ideas. In
the passage under discussion there is not one word about the existence
of things when they are not perceived by us. Philonous speaks of
depriving the world "of all reality," of reducing it to "a false imaginary glare," of the "real existence" of things, and of inferring God's
existence from "the bare existence of the sensible world."

Berkeley makes Philonous say that Hylas's scepticism arises
precisely from his misunderstanding of what it is for something to be
real; and we have already noted Berkeley's insistence that, properly
understood, the notion of "a real thing" is the notion of something
which exists *although not caused by me*, and is not the notion of
something which exists *when not perceived by me*.

Secondly, consider how the passage develops. Hylas asks whether
Philonous's position differs from "a notion entertained by some eminent moderns, of seeing all things in God." The discussion then
becomes mired in Philonous's attempt to understand and to criticise
Malebranche; until finally Philonous brushes Malebranche aside and
pulls the discussion back to his own views with the abrupt words:
"Take here in brief my meaning. . . .," whereupon he launches into a
lucid presentation of the passivity argument!

Why have some commentators associated the "false imaginary
glare" passage with the continuity argument, in the face of such clear
indications that this is a mistake? There are two sentences which, I
suspect, have had a special responsibility for the misconstruction of the
passage as a whole. Philonous says: "To me it is evident, for the
reasons you allow of, that sensible things cannot exist otherwise than in
a mind or spirit. Whence I conclude, not that they have no real
existence, but that seeing they depend not on my thought, and have an
existence distinct from being perceived by me, there must be some
other mind wherein they exist." Since the first sentence is explicitly
concerned with the ownership of ideas, it might be argued that the
second sentence concerns ownership too, so that the two together do
introduce the continuity argument.

Since this reading of the two sentences makes nonsense of the rest of the passage, I do not think that anyone could *easily* accept it unless he had already overlooked all Berkeley's distinctions between the two sorts of scepticism which go with the two arguments for God's existence. In fact, though, the interpretation in question is probably wrong. At the beginning of the paragraph, Philonous says that his opinions *would* lead to the sceptical conclusion that sensible things are not real *if* Hylas were right in taking "the reality of sensible things" to consist in "an absolute existence out of the minds of spirits." He goes on: "But I neither said nor thought the reality of sensible things was to be defined after that manner. To me it is evident, for the reasons you allow of, that sensible things cannot exist otherwise than in a mind or spirit. Whence I conclude . . . etc." The argument is not that sensible things cannot exist out of all minds, but do sometimes exist out of human minds and must therefore sometimes exist in a non-human mind. It is that sensible things cannot exist out of all minds, but are undoubtedly real, and therefore "real" must be defined in some other way than "capable of existing out of all minds." The point about the ownership of ideas comes in here solely in order to highlight Hylas's wrong analysis of "real."

I do not contend that the passage is flawless. On my interpretation, Philonous's "Whence I conclude . . ." is too abrupt: there should at this point be a reference to the analysis of "real" which Philonous does accept. But if we are to take the passage as giving the continuity argument, then—apart from the difficulties already mentioned—we must suppose that in Berkeley's first and almost his only presentation of that argument he fails to make the crucial point that something may exist out of all human minds without existing out of all minds whatsoever.

If someone still insists that in this passage Berkeley is nevertheless also thinking of the continuity argument and conflating it with the passivity argument, I cannot prove him wrong. In an earlier section I listed all but four of Berkeley's uses of "depend" and its cognates in speaking of the relationship between ideas and minds. Of the four exceptions, one was in sec. 56 where Berkeley criticises an argument which turns upon the ambiguity of "depend"; one was in *Principles* sec. 146 where Berkeley himself exploits the ambiguity in order to move from "every idea depends upon (= is owned by) a mind" to "every idea depends upon (= is caused by) a mind": and one was in the third dialogue, p. 193, where Berkeley exploits the ambiguity in reverse, in his one clear presentation of the continuity argument. The fourth use of "depend" which was omitted from my lists is the one now under discussion, and it may be that this too should be treated as a mixed use of "depend," in which it does two things at once. But at least let it be recognised that in this case the mixture is quite different from the other three: each of the latter is clearly and explicitly concerned both with the ownership and with the causation of ideas, and the ambiguity of "depend" explains how the two things are brought together. In the "false imaginary glare" passage, however, the only explicit reference to ownership admits of a perfectly good explanation as relevant to the criticism of Hylas's definition of "real": there is no *need* to say that "depend" is used ambiguously here, except the need created by an antecedent prejudice in favour of taking this passage to express the continuity argument.

THE ANSWERS TO QUESTIONS (2) AND (4)

Berkeley addresses himself to (a) the accusation that on his principles the sensible world is robbed of its reality, and (b) the accusation that on his principles the sensible world flickers in and out of existence. He cares deeply about (a), and is at great pains to rebut it by an account of the correct meaning of "real," an account which, since it defines "real" only for ideas which one *does* have, has no bearing on the question of whether any ideas exist which one does not have. Not only is Berkeley manifestly anxious to rebut (a), but he also takes this to be the focus of the one argument which he strenuously advances for the existence of God.

His treatment of (b), apart from two sentences in the third dialogue, is uniformly relaxed and agnostic. He would as soon say that (b) is meaningless as say that (b) does not follow from his principles; he rests no weight on the claim that he is not committed to (b); and he most certainly does not—with the one tiny exception already noted—argue from the falsity of (b) to the existence of God.

My second and fourth questions, then, may be answered as follows. Berkeley makes so little of the continuity argument, and is so silent about its relationship to the passivity argument, because he does not seriously wish to employ the continuity argument at all. Not only is Berkeley uninterested in arguing from the continuity of objects to the existence of God; he is not even interested in arguing strenuously from the existence of God to the possible continuity of objects. Those who think otherwise—those who accept the limericks' account of Berkeley's thought on continuity—have not attended carefully enough to what he actually wrote.

University of Cambridge.

BERKELEY AND THE TREE
IN THE QUAD*

E. J. Furlong

Why did Berkeley believe that the tree continues to be when no one's about in the quad? Or, to quote from Mr. Jonathan Bennett's stimulating and provocative article ("Berkeley and God," *Philosophy* July 1965), "Why does Berkeley, in the continuity argument (for God's existence), allow himself the premiss that objects exist while not perceived by any human?" Mr. Bennett continues: "A possible answer is that this is such a deep-rooted, normal human assumption that Berkeley could not help making it even though he could not, on his own philosophical principles, be entitled to make it. . . . This strikes me as false. In many places, Berkeley calmly says that if we clear our minds we shall see that we have no grounds for believing in the existence of objects while they are unperceived." And Mr. Bennett refers to *Principles* § 4 and § 6, quoting from the latter a passage which ends ". . . they must either have no existence at all, or else subsist in the mind of some eternal spirit." "These are not the words of someone," Mr. Bennett comments, "who would add that since objects do exist when not perceived by created spirits therefore there must be an eternal spirit which perceives them."

Mr. Bennett also refers to Principles § 45–8 where Berkeley discusses at length the intermittency objection to his philosophy. We might well think—before we had considered Mr. Bennett's arguments—that in these paragraphs Berkeley's procedure is as follows: first, he asks, has not his *esse est percipi* been proved to the hilt, no matter how strange its consequences? then (§§ 46–7) he argues *ad hominem* that other theories are certainly liable to the intermittency objection; but finally (§ 48), having played sufficiently with the objection, he acts on his note-books maxim to "bring the killing blow at the last": rounding on his objector he declares that the objection does not in fact do any damage to the Berkeleian theory. "For tho we hold indeed the objects

---

* From *Philosophy*, XLI (1966), 169–173. Reprinted by permission of the author and the editors of *Philosophy*.

161

of sense to be nothing else but ideas which cannot exist unperceiv'd: yet we may not hence conclude they have no existence except only while they are perceiv'd by us, since there may be some other spirit that perceives them, tho we do not. . . . It does not therefore follow from the foregoing principles, that bodies are annihilated and created every moment." Mr. Bennett, however, takes a different view of § 48. "The crucial expressions," he writes, "are 'we may not hence *conclude*,' 'there *may* be some other spirit,' 'it does not therefore *follow*.' These are not the words of someone who proposes to base the continuity argument on the absurdity of denying that objects have a continuous existence" (italics Mr. Bennett's). In fact, "Berkeley resolutely, and mockingly, refuses to say that it [intermittency] is absurd."

Mr. Bennett considers that we have to wait till the third of the *Three dialogues* for an *argument* by Berkeley that objects continue to be when unperceived by us. In the *Principles* Berkeley "cares deeply about" the "reality" of sensible things but their continuity is "not for him a matter of urgency or anxiety or even much interest."

Now Mr. Bennett is certainly right in claiming that in the *Principles* Berkeley does not state his continuity argument for God's existence: he gives only what Mr. Bennett calls his "passivity argument"—the argument to God as the cause of the "continual succession of ideas" (§ 26). We have to wait till the *Three dialogues* for a statement of the continuity argument. But is Mr. Bennett correct in his view that Berkeley, when writing the *Principles*, did not care very much about the continuity of sensible things? "There *may* be some other spirit." Is the "may" a casual, detached, for-all-I-care "may"? or is it a suggestive "may," a "may" of understatement, of confidence— the quizzical "may" of the man who knows the way out of the maze, "You *may* get out if you try that path"?

Was Berkeley unconcerned about intermittency?

At this point one naturally enquires, do Berkeley's note-books throw any light on our query? Do they indicate whether he is likely to have used a casual "may," as Mr. Bennett argues, or a suggestive "may," as others have thought? The note-books have numerous references to the topic. But before we consider them there is a general point that may be conveniently made here. Berkeley was certainly anxious to show in both his *Principles* and his *Three dialogues*, that his system took nothing from the reality of things—and he was rightly anxious, as the reactions of such plain men as Dr. Johnson were to show. Now a plain man, offered a currant bun which he was assured by Berkeley was perfectly real, would be somewhat uneasy if he were also informed that on Berkeley's philosophy the bun had an intermittent existence. How can I digest it? How will it nourish me? he might well ask. It is *prima facie* hardly likely that Berkeley should be concerned about the reality of sensible things, but indifferent to their continuity. And we might note that one of his criteria for the real as opposed to the imaginary is constancy (*Principles* § 33). Constancy is not the same thing as continuity, but they are near allied.

To return now to the note-books evidence. Here is a list of the relevant entries:[1] 198, 185, 185a, 194, 293a, 408, 424a, 429, 429a, 472, 473, 477a, 801, 802. These entries refer directly to our topic; others bear on it indirectly. Berkeley's thought on the subject, as on many other subjects during that remarkable year of discovery when his note-books were written, shows a striking development, indeed revolution—an instance of what Dr. Luce has recently called "the dialectic of immaterialism." Let us look at typical landmarks in the journey.

+ On account of my doctrine the identity of finite substances must consist in something else than continued existence, or relation to determin'd time and place of beginning to exist, the existence of our thoughts which being combin'd make all substances) being frequently interrupted, & they having divers beginnings, & endings.

(Entry 194)

+ Bodies taken for Powers do exist when not perceiv'd but this existence is not actual. When I say a power exists no more is meant than that if in the light I open my eyes & look that way I shall see it i.e. the body &c.

(Entry 293a)

M or rather why he [a Cartesian] supposes all the Matter, for bodies & their qualitys I do allow to exist independently of Our mind.

(Entry 477a)

P I differ from the Cartesians in that I make extension, Colour etc to exist really in Bodies & independent of Our Mind. All these carefully & lucidly to be set forth.

(Entry 801)

MP Not to mention the Combinations of Powers but to say the things the effects themselves to really exist even when not actually perceiv'd but still with relation to perception.

(Entry 802)

---

[1] References are to A. A. Luce diplomatic edition, *Berkeley's Philosophical Commentaries*, 1944. Hereafter, *P.C.*

The import of these entries is not hard to see. Entry 194 shows Berkeley clearly committed to intermittency. Entry 293a allows a hypothetical, non-actual existence to bodies when not perceived. Their actual existence is still intermittent. But, it will be observed, both these entries have the marginal sign +, which means "reject."[2] And when we come to entry 477a we find that Berkeley is, by implication, distinguishing between "Our mind" and—though he does not say so, but what else can it be?—God's mind. When he writes entry 801 he is allowing an actual existence even to colours "independent of Our Mind." And entry 802 is a direct repudiation of the hypothetical existence view stated in 293a.

It is plain then that at the end of his note-book thinking Berkeley was quite sure that the tree continues to be when no one's about in the quad. He had found a way, by distinguishing between our mind and some other mind, of having the best of both worlds—of "siding with the Mob" and at the same time retaining *esse est percipi*. When he had written his "intermittency entries" 194 and 293a it had looked as if *esse est percipi* and the commonsense belief in non-intermittency were incompatible. Now he has found, to his relief, that they are compatible. And he states this achievement as a point in his favour as compared with the Cartesians. This is not the claim of one who was unconcerned about intermittency. It follows that when Berkeley says in the *Principles* passage we were discussing, "we may not hence conclude they have no existence except only while they are perceiv'd by us," he would have been quite prepared to substitute "we must not hence conclude" for "we may not hence conclude"; and when he writes "since there may be some other spirit that perceives them tho we do not," his "may" is not, as Mr. Bennett asserts, a casual, indifferent "may" but rather a suggestive "may," Socratically ironic. Or possibly we should put the matter in a slightly different way. Berkeley, towards the end of his note-books, had found, as we saw, that to accept *esse est percipi* does not imply giving up commonsense. There is no inference from *esse est percipi* to intermittency. "We *may* not hence conclude . . ." The "may" was good enough for him. It ruled out the objectionable inference. He would indeed have been prepared to go further, and put "must" for "may," but, with his fine sense of logic and drama, he used the minimum term the context needed.

We have seen how Berkeley's thought on intermittency changed

2 P.C., pp. xxv ff.

in his note-books to the position he was to publish in the *Principles*. But the change did not stop there. As we noted already, we have to wait till the *Three dialogues* for the continuity argument. We might chart the whole process of thinking in the following stages:

Note-book entries 194, 293a: intermittency allowed to be a consequence of *esse est percipi* (c. autumn 1707). Note-book entries 801, 802 and *Principles* § 48: intermittency denied to be a consequence of *esse est percipi* because God may perceive things when we do not; i.e. God exists (why? the passivity argument) and may perceive when we do not, therefore there is no clash between *esse est percipi* and commonsense (c. summer 1708–spring 1710). *Three dialogues* (*Works*, ed. Luce and Jessop, vol. 2, pp. 230–1): intermittency is false, continuity is true, i.e. commonsense is to be accepted, therefore God exists (c. 1712–13).

We might put the process of thought this way. First, commonsense and *esse est percipi* are believed to clash; since *esse est percipi* is intuitively true, commonsense must go (P.C. 194, 293a: there is an echo of this assertion in *Principles* § 45). Then it is seen that commonsense can be rescued (P.C. 801, 802, *Principles* § 48). Finally it is claimed that commonsense can be used as a premiss. We have in turn the relations of exclusion, compatibility and entailment.

[It should, perhaps, be added that Berkeley's commonsense belief in the continuity of objects did not prevent him from offering, by implication, a highly-refined analysis of what this continuity consists in: *Works*, vol. 2, pp. 245–8. He does, indeed, claim that his account of sameness in this connexion does not "deviate either from propriety of language or the truth of things." He may be unduly hopeful here; still, what in fact does the plain man believe about the colour of the leaves on the tree in the quad when unobserved, or at 3 A.M.?]

What right had Berkeley to his belief in the continuity of objects?

What I have so far been mainly concerned to argue, as against Mr. Bennett, is that when Berkeley wrote the *Principles* he did believe in, and care about, the continuity of objects. But there is also the question of logic: what right had Berkeley to his commonsense belief in continuity? Does he offer any argument to support his position? We might well think that he does not. But Mr. Bennett points out that in the *Three dialogues* statement of the continuity argument Berkeley does give a reason for his belief in continuity. "It is plain," says Philonous, "they [sensible things] have an existence exterior to my mind, since I find them by experience to be independent of it. There is therefore some other mind wherein they exist, during the intervals between the times of my perceiving them." Berkeley here infers from "independent of my mind," i.e. not produced by me, to existing unperceived by me. (It is an argument from what Hume will call "distinct" existence to "continued" existence.) The argument is indeed very shaky, but an argument it is, and Mr. Bennett has rendered a service in drawing attention to it and to the ambiguities in the verb "depend" which Berkeley's reasoning at key-points exhibits. (Bennett, op. cit., pp. 212, 215).

Did Berkeley clearly distinguish in the Principles *and* Three dialogues *two arguments for the existence of God?*

Mr. Bennett asks why, if continuity were important to Berkeley, he makes so little of the continuity argument for God's existence, devoting in all but two (or three) sentences to it. The "false imaginary glare" passage in the second of the *Three dialogues*, Mr. Bennett holds, includes a statement, not of the continuity argument, but of the passivity argument: Berkeley here, as elsewhere, is much more concerned with the reality of sensible things, explained by reference to their production, than with their continuity. Mr. Bennett does allow, indeed, that "if someone still insists that in this passage Berkeley is nevertheless also thinking of the continuity argument and conflating it with the passivity argument, I cannot prove him wrong." Prompted by this concession, I think we might wonder whether Berkeley was aware explicitly of the continuity and passivity arguments as two separate proofs or whether he did not think of them as two complementary pieces of reasoning. The continuity argument, he might have thought, puts the stress on perceiving, the passivity argument on willing. And we know from the protracted debate in his second note-book how closely connected he held perceiving, or thinking, and willing, to be. The three-sentence statement of the continuity argument, where the stress is on perception, concludes that there is an omnipresent eternal Mind, which "knows and comprehends all things and *exhibits them to our view* . . ." (italics mine). The conclusion is to both a knowing and an active or willing being—to a conserver as well as a creator. If I am right in suggesting that Berkeley did not think of the continuity argument as clearly different from the passivity argument this would explain why he does not draw special attention to the former.[3]

[3] Cf. Sillem, E. A., *George Berkeley and the Proofs for the Existence of God* (chapter 6), London: Longmans, 1957.

To sum up—the main points I have made are as follows:

1. Mr. Bennett asserts that in the *Principles* Berkeley shows little concern for the continuity of sensible things, their non-intermittent existence. I have argued that his note-books show *per contra*, that while he began by accepting intermittency as an implication of *esse est percipi* he came to see—with relief—that the implication could be avoided: he could both hold on to the intuitive truth of *esse est percipi* and also accept the continuity of sensible things. This is the position he adopted in the *Principles*. In the *Three dialogues* he goes further, and uses the continuity of objects as a premiss from which to infer the existence of God.

2. I accept Mr. Bennett's point that in the *Three dialogues* Berkeley gives an argument, though not a valid one, for the continuity of objects.

3. I have suggested that Berkeley saw the continuity and passivity arguments as two complementary portions of the one proof, rather than as two separate pieces of reasoning.

University of Dublin.

SUGGESTED FURTHER READINGS

Although several bibliographies on the writings of George Berkeley are available, we list here only a few works and some books and articles that may be used by students to extend their study of *The Principles of Human Knowledge*.

SELECTED WORKS OF BERKELEY

Philosophical Commentaries (1707–8). Vol. I of *The Works of George Berkeley, Bishop of Cloyne*, ed. A. A. Luce and T. E. Jessop. London: Nelson, 1948.

An Essay Towards a New Theory of Vision. Dublin, 1709.

A Treatise Concerning the Principles of Human Knowledge. Part I. Dublin, 1710.

Three Dialogues Between Hylas and Philonous. London, 1713.

De Motu. London, 1721.

Alciphron; or, The Minute Philosopher. London & Dublin, 1732.

Theory of Vision Vindicated. London, 1733.

The Analyst: or a Discourse Addressed to an Infidel Mathematician. Dublin and London, 1734.

The Principles of Human Knowledge (revised) and *Three Dialogues Between Hylas and Philonous.* London, 1734.

The Querist. Dublin and London, 1735–37.

Siris. Dublin and London, 1744.

Recent inexpensive editions of *The Principles of Human Knowledge*:

A Treatise Concerning the Principles of Human Knowledge, ed. C. M. Turbayne. New York: Bobbs-Merrill Company, Inc., Library of Liberal Arts, 1957.

The Principles of Human Knowledge (with other writings), ed. G. J. Warnock. London: The Fontana Library, Collins, 1962; and Cleveland: World Publishing Company, Meridian Books, 1963.

Berkeley's Philosophical Writings, ed. D. M. Armstrong. New York: Collier, 1965.

GENERAL BOOKS AND ARTICLES ON BERKELEY AND HIS PHILOSOPHY

Armstrong, D. M. *Berkeley's Theory of Vision.* Melbourne: Melbourne University Press, 1960.

Fraser, A. C. *Berkeley*. Edinburgh: Blackwood's Philosophical Classics, 1881.

Johnston, G. A. *The Development of Berkeley's Philosophy*. London: Macmillan, 1923.

Luce, A. A. *The Life of George Berkeley*. London: Nelson, 1949.

————. *The Dialectic of Immaterialism*. London: Hodder and Stoughton, Ltd., 1963.

Mill, J. S. "Berkeley's Life and Writings," in his *Three Essays on Religion*. New York: Henry Holt & Co., 1874, pp. 261–302.

Warnock, G. J. *Berkeley*. London: Penguin Books, 1953.

BICENTENARY CELEBRATION PUBLICATIONS ON BERKELEY AND HIS PHILOSOPHY

British Journal for the Philosophy of Science (Edinburgh). Vol. 4, No. 13, 1953.

George Berkeley, ed. S. Pepper, K. Aschenbrenner, and B. Mates. Berkeley: University of California Publications in Philosophy, Vol. 29, 1957.

Hermathena (Trinity College, Dublin). No. 82, 1953.

Revue Internationale de Philosophie (Brussels). Vol. 7, Nos. 23–24, 1953.

Revue Philosophie (Paris). Vol. 143, April–June 1953.

CRITICAL ESSAYS

Minds and Ideas

Aschenbrenner, K. "Bishop Berkeley on Existence in the Mind," in *George Berkeley*, ed. S. Pepper, K. Aschenbrenner, and B. Mates. Berkeley: University of California Publications in Philosophy, 29 (1957), 37–64.

Braybrooke, D. "The Numerical Identity of Ideas," *The Philosophical Review*, LXIV (1955), 631–636.

Cummins, P. D. "Berkeley's Likeness Principle," *Journal of the History of Philosophy*, IV, No. 1 (1966), 63–69.

Datta, D. M. "Berkeley's Objective Idealism: An Indian View," in *New Studies in Berkeley's Philosophy*, Warren E. Steinkraus, ed. New York: Holt, Rinehart and Winston, Inc., 1966.

Davis, J. W. "Berkeley's Doctrine of the Notion," *The Review of Metaphysics*, XII (1959), 378–389.

Fritz, Anita D. "Berkeley's Self—Its Origin in Malebranche," *Journal of the History of Ideas*, XV (1954), 554–572.

Furlong, E. J. "Abstract Ideas and Images," *Aristotelian Society Supplementary Volume*, XXVII (1953), 121–136.

Grey, D. "Berkeley on Other Selves: A Study in Fugue," *Philosophical Quarterly*, IV (1954), 28–44.

———. "The Solipsism of Bishop Berkeley," *Philosophical Quarterly*, II (1952), 338–349.

Grossman, R. "Digby and Berkeley on Notions," *Theoria*, XXVI (1960), 17–30.

Hay, W. H. "Berkeley's Argument from Nominalism," *Revue Internationale de Philosophie*, VII (1953), 1–9.

James, William. " 'Abstract' Ideas," in *The Principles of Psychology*. New York: Henry Holt & Co., 1890, pp. 468–482.

———. "Some Metaphysical Problems Pragmatically Considered," Lecture III in *Pragmatism, A New Name for Some Old Ways of Thinking*. New York: Longmans, Green & Co., 1907.

Martin, R. M. "On the Berkeley-Russell Theory of Proper Names," *Philosophy and Phenomenological Research*, XIII (1952–53), 221–231.

Rome, S. C. "Berkeley's Conceptualism," *The Philosophical Review*, XV (1946), 680–686.

Tipton, I. C. "Berkeley's View of Spirit," in *New Studies in Berkeley's Philosophy*, Warren E. Steinkraus ed. New York: Holt, Rinehart and Winston, Inc., 1966.

White, A. R. "The Ambiguity of Berkeley's 'Without the Mind,' " *Hermathena*, No. 83 (May 1954), pp. 55–65.

Perception and Existence

Allaire, E. B. "Berkeley's Idealism," *Theoria*, XXVIII–XXIX (1962–63), 229–244.

Armstrong, D. M. "Refutations of Phenomenalism" in *Perception and the External World*. New York: Humanities Press, 1961.

Berlin, I. "Empirical Propositions and Hypothetical Statements," *Mind*, LIX (1950), 289–312.

Broad, C. D. "Berkeley's Denial of Maternal Substance," *The Philosophical Review*, LXIII, 2 (April 1954), 155–181.

———. "Berkeley's Argument about Material Substance," *The Proceedings of the British Academy*, XXVIII (1942), 119–138.

Brunton, J. A. "Berkeley and the External World," *Philosophy*, XXVIII (1953), 325–341.

Carter, W. B. "Some Problems of the Relation between Berkeley's New Theory of Vision and His Principles," *Ratio*, III, No. 2 (1961), 174–192.

Cummins, P. S. "Perceptual Reliability and Ideas," *Philosophy and Phenomenological Research*, XXIV (1963), 202–214.

Doney, Willis. "Two Questions about Berkeley," *The Philosophical Review*, LXI (1952), pp. 382–391.

Fain, Haskell. "More on the *Esse Est Percipi*–Principle," *Theoria*, XXV (1959), 65–81.

Hallett, H. F. "Dr. Johnson's Refutation of Bishop Berkeley," *Mind*, XVI (1947), 132–147.

Kantonen, T. A. "The Influence of Descartes on Berkeley," *The Philosophical Review*, III (1934), pp. 483–500.

Marc-Wogau, K. "Some Remarks on Haskell Fain's paper 'More on the *Esse Est Percipi*–Principle,'" *Theoria*, XXV (1959), 115–117.

————. "The Argument from Illusion and Berkeley's Idealism," *Theoria*, XXIV (1958), 94–106.

Margolis, Joseph. "*Esse Est Percipi* Once Again," *Dialogue*, V, No. 4 (March 1967), 516–524.

Mates, B. "Berkeley Was Right," in *George Berkeley*, ed. S. Pepper, K. Aschenbrenner, and B. Mates. Berkeley: University of California Publications in Philosophy, 29 (1957), 158–174.

Miles, T. R. "Berkeley and Ryle: Some Comparisons," *Philosophy*, XXVIII (1953), 58–71.

Moore, G. E. "Sense Data and Physical Objects," in *The Commonplace Book of G. E. Moore, 1919–1953*, ed. C. Lewy. London: George Allen & Unwin, Ltd., 1963.

Murphy, J. G. "Berkeley and the Metaphor of Mental Substance," *Ratio*, VII, No. 2 (1965), 170–179.

Peirce, C. S. "Critical Review of Berkeley's Idealism," *North American Review*, 93 (Oct. 1871), 449–472.

Phillips, Robert L. "Discussion: Austin and Berkeley on Perception," *Philosophy*, XXXIX (1964), 161–163.

Prior, A. N. "Berkeley on Logical Form," *Theoria*, XXI (1955), 117–122.

Rome, S. C. "The Scottish Refutation of Berkeley's Immaterialism," *Philosophy and Phenomenological Research*, III, No. 3 (March 1943), 313–325.

Stock, J. L. "What Did Berkeley Mean by *Esse Is Percipi?*" *Mind*, XLV (1936), 310–323.

Sullivan, C. J. "Berkeley's Attack on Matter," in *George Berkeley*, ed. S. Pepper, K. Aschenbrenner, and B. Mates. Berkeley: University of California Publications in Philosophy, 29 (1957), 20–36.

Warnock, G. F. "Empirical Propositions and Hypothetical Statements," *Mind*, LIX (1950), 289–312.

Philosophy and Science

Turbayne, C. M. "Berkeley and Russell on Space," *Dialectica* (1954), pp. 210–227.

Withrow, G. J. "Berkeley's Philosophy of Motion," *British Journal for the Philosophy of Science*, IV (1953–54), 37–45.

Primary and Secondary Qualities

Adams, E. M. "Primary and Secondary Qualities," *Journal of Philosophy*, XLV, No. 16 (1948), 435–442.

Brain, W. R. *Mind, Perception, and Science.* Oxford: Blackwell Scientific Publications, Blackwell's, 1951.

Brittan, G. G. "Primary and Secondary Qualities," Dissertation, Stanford University, 1966.

Chisholm, R. M. "Secondary Qualities," in *Perceiving: A Philosophical Study.* Ithaca, New York: Cornell University Press, 1957, pp. 126–141.

Hirst, R. V. *The Problems of Perception*, Chapters I–VI. London: G. Allen & Unwin, 1959.

Kneale, W. C. "Sensations and the Physical World," *Philosophical Quarterly*, I, No. 2 (1951), 109–126.

Ryle, Gilbert. *Dilemmas.* Cambridge: Cambridge University Press, 1954.

Smart, J. C. "Colours," *Philosophy*, XXXVI, No. 137 (1961), 128–142.

The Existence of God

Hurlbutt, R. H. "Berkeley's Theology," in *George Berkeley*, ed. S. Pepper, K. Aschenbrenner, and B. Mates. Berkeley: University of California Publications in Philosophy, 29 (1957), 106–121.

Mabbott, J. D. "The Place of God in Berkeley's Philosophy," *Philosophy*, VI (1931), 18–29.